Twilight Realm
A Tarot of Faery

Twilight Realm
A Tarot of Faery

Beth Wilder

4880 Lower Valley Road, Atglen, Pennsylvania 19310

Schiffer Books are available at special discounts for bulk purchases for sales promotions or premiums. Special editions, including personalized covers, corporate imprints, and excerpts can be created in large quantities for special needs. For more information contact the publisher:

Published by Schiffer Publishing Ltd.
4880 Lower Valley Road
Atglen, PA 19310
Phone: (610) 593-1777; Fax: (610) 593-2002
E-mail: Info@schifferbooks.com

For the largest selection of fine reference books on this and related subjects, please visit our web site at **www.schifferbooks.com**
We are always looking for people to write books on new and related subjects. If you have an idea for a book please contact us at the above address.

This book may be purchased from the publisher.
Include $5.00 for shipping.
Please try your bookstore first.
You may write for a free catalog.

In Europe, Schiffer books are distributed by
Bushwood Books
6 Marksbury Ave.
Kew Gardens
Surrey TW9 4JF England
Phone: 44 (0) 20 8392-8585; Fax: 44 (0) 20 8392-9876
E-mail: info@bushwoodbooks.co.uk
Website: www.bushwoodbooks.co.uk

Designed by RoS
Type set in Bible ScrT/Century Oldst BT

ISBN: 978-0-7643-3393-4

Printed in China

All artwork and text courtesy of Beth Wilder.

Dedication

This deck is dedicated to all the nature spirits that have inhabited and helped care for the earth since its creation. Too often you have gone unrecognized simply because our human eyes are seldom capable of beholding your ethereal presence. Thank you for the times you have made yourselves known to us and for the lessons you have imparted to us, even though we may never have been aware of what you were doing at the time. Thank you for helping take care of the planet and for sharing your many gifts with us. Hopefully, one day more people will be graced with the knowledge of your existence and will learn to give back as much to you as you have given to us.

Acknowledgments

I wish to thank my entire family for their unwavering encouragement of my artistic abilities since I was a child. I would not be who I am without them, and no one could ask for a more loving and supportive family. I would especially like to thank my sister, Lisa, and my nieces, Heather and Hilary (who really are the sunshine of my life!), for allowing their images to be included in my deck.

I would also like to thank the following friends who appear in one form or another throughout this deck: Jennifer Wilson, Mark Raymer, Malinda Wickham, Kim Burton, Krista Biggs, Brad Nelson, Pat Wilder, and Pam Ware.

So many friends contributed to my life in ways that ultimately assisted in the outcome of this deck, but some are truly outstanding. I wish to thank Lydia Gossman for gifting me with my first set of Tarot cards, Shelia Hall for helping me understand more about how the cards work, Pam Ware for helping me become more attuned to the natural world and being the best friend I could ever ask for, and Thomas Freese for appearing in my life just in time to encourage and help me with the editing of this book.

Two people deserve special recognition, because without them this deck most likely would never have come to fruition. Mark Raymer, who shares my love for the Faery Realm and who has patiently listened to my thoughts on every possible subject, even when he felt left out somewhere "in the painted desert." Most of all, I wish to thank Jennifer Wilson, who instilled in me a real appreciation for Tarot decks, not only for their artwork, but for the significance of their meanings and what I could learn from them. Without Jennifer's constant encouragement, I would never have spent ten years drawing pictures for a Tarot deck in the hopes of one day having it published. And I certainly cannot forget Dinah Roseberry and Schiffer Publishing for giving me this wonderful opportunity to share my Tarot deck with the world.

Last, but definitely not least, I would like to thank the love of my life, Gary Hoofnel, for being there and having faith in me.

Contents

Introduction

As soon as I began collecting tarot cards many years ago, I realized how helpful they were in stimulating the mind and meditating on life's questions. I thought a personalized deck would mean even more to me, since I would know the inherent meaning of the symbols I used when designing the cards. I started work on a deck for my use alone, but friends discovered what I was doing and wanted to take part in its creation. Although it sounded like a nice idea, I soon realized that "too many cooks spoil the broth." The deck I started out to make became a confusing amalgam of ideas and images, so I decided to just give up on the notion.

I was not happy about letting go of the conception of my own deck. One night, as I lay in the darkness of my room, I pondered all this, wondering what I could possibly do. Suddenly a magical occurrence befell me. I saw tiny sparks of light around my face, accompanied by gentle breezes and soft caresses. I heard delicate tinkling whispers, "Do it about us. Let us be in it. We want to help. Do it about us."

The fairies were asking me to create a tarot deck about them!

This may sound strange to those who do not believe in fairies and other spirits, but I *do* believe in them whole-heartedly and I always have. I take the things they show me and teach me very seriously, or at least as seriously as fairies *want* people to take them. When they asked to be part of this deck, I knew they had good reason.

Now this deck has taken on a different meaning for me. I have not made it for my use alone. I have made it as a way for the fairies to communicate with other people because that is what they asked of me. So this deck is a gift from the world of Faery to those individuals wise enough to understand that fairies are all around us. They help us in sometimes baffling or confounding ways, but their true intent is to impart lessons that encourage our growth.

The images in this deck represent different types of fairies. Some of them have come to me in dreams, while others were seen by me in a waking state. In each case, I have noted the circumstances in the cards' descriptions. Many of the images, however, I simply created from fairy lore using the particular type of fairy I thought would be appropriate to the meaning of each card.

I apologize ahead of time to Tarot enthusiasts who are used to cards appearing in certain ways with specific symbols and meanings attached to them. These cards were inspired by the fairies around me, and they may not reflect typical Tarot ideology. For example, I was led to associate the suit of Swords with the element of Fire and the suit of

Wands with the element of Air. The logic behind this decision lies in the fact that dwarves craft swords using the element of fire while sylphs that inhabit the air are most likely to be portrayed with wands. Another difference is that the suit typically referred to as Pentacles or Coins, I have decided to call "Rings," out of respect for Faery Rings. The "Knight" cards are herein represented by 2 Princes and 2 Princesses for no other reason than that it just felt right to me at the time.

These cards should be used in whatever manner the reader feels most comfortable. For those who have never used a Tarot deck before, it is wise to become acquainted with the cards before using them the first time. Contemplating each card is one way to attune to them. Holding the cards while envisioning pure, light energy entering them is another way to center one's focus and keep away any negative forces that might interfere with a reading.

Shuffling the deck is a matter best left to the individual. Some people prefer to shuffle the cards a set number of times while others simply shuffle the deck until it feels right. Since these cards were designed with reversed meanings, it does not matter if some cards are turned upside-down while shuffling. It is very important, however, that the reader focus on the question to be answered while shuffling the cards. If the reader's intent is not clear while shuffling, the cards typically refuse to work well because they assume the reading is not being taken seriously.

Once the cards have been shuffled to one's satisfaction while concentrating on a question, a quick answer may be obtained by drawing a card from the top of the deck. Some people feel drawn to remove cards from within the deck, which is just as good. Again, the reader should always do what feels most comfortable. If a card happens to fall from the deck while it is being shuffled, pay special attention – that card wants to be heard.

While one card is often enough to answer a question, many Tarot readers prefer to go more in depth. Card layouts can become quite complex depending on one's level of skill at reading the spreads, and many books exist which go into great detail on the subject. For those who are advanced Tarot readers, I recommend using whatever card layouts you typically prefer to use. For those who are not so adept at reading tarot spreads, or for those who would like a quicker and easier way to read the answers to their questions, I suggest the methods of reading the cards that follows.

Tarot Spreads

The Three Card Spread

The Three Card Spread provides the reader with a series of cards that represent past, present, and future in regard to the question posed. Remember to ask open-ended questions when using the cards, rather than ones that need a "yes" or "no" answer. Tarot cards like to be informative, and most of the time, there is far more to a situation than can be explained by a simple "yes" or "no" answer.

The first two cards in this spread correspond to events related to the question at hand insofar as the past and present are concerned. The final card signifies the future outcome. When doing a Tarot reading, always bear in mind that the future is not set in stone. If a card is drawn that seems disturbing, do not assume that events will turn out for the worst. Free will is a greater determining factor in our lives than anything else because we have control over our own will. A seemingly negative card could merely be a wake-up call to alert the reader that more attention needs to be paid to the situation.

Past

Present

Future

The Star Spread

This is a method I use to double check a reading that may not have been clear enough to me the first time. When using this spread, I carefully rephrase my question as I shuffle and lay out the cards.

I depend on **cards 1 and 2** to reflect the gist of my question so I know I am on the right track.

Cards 3 and 4 are meant to explain the situation in more depth.

Card 5 will hopefully provide me with the outcome of the question at hand.

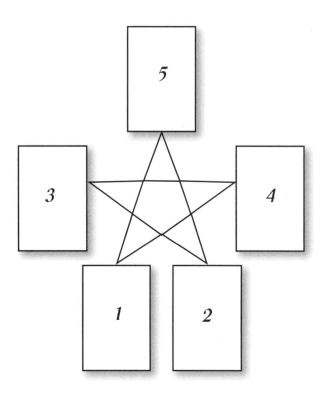

The Elements Spread

I have found this spread to work very well with this particular deck. I've named it the Elements Spread since this deck encompasses the elements of earth, air, fire, water, and ether. I also see in this layout the four directions, with the central card representing what is within. I read the cards in the following manner:

Card 1 represents the ethereal realm of Faery. It denotes the heart of the matter, especially as it pertains to oneself.

Card 2 represents the north, the element of air, and the intellect in regard to the question at hand.

Card 3 represents the south, the element of earth, and family in regard to the stated question.

Card 4 represents the east, the element of water, and illumination – especially concerning one's emotions – in regard to the question posed.

Card 5 represents the west, the element of fire, and the future in regard to the question posed.

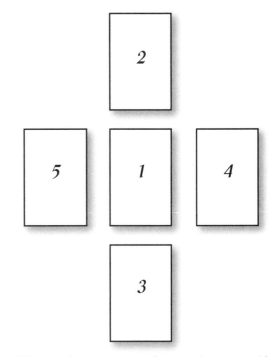

These are just some suggestions as to how to use this deck. Open your mind and heart, and no doubt the denizens of Faery will give you even more ideas.

I now present to you a gift from Faery. I hope you learn as much while using these cards as I did making them.

And now, prepare to enter a world of enchantment. Step into the Twilight Realm...

Major Arcana

XX Judgment

XV The De

XXI The World

XIV Temperance

XVIII The Moon

O- The FOOL

Meaning: *Complete folly. Happiness. Letting go. Change of circumstances or environment. Fearlessness. Lack of logic. Not using one's head.*

This little fellow appeared to me one day when I was experimenting with drawing fairies in my room. I could not see with my eyes, but did "see" with my inner vision. I simply held the pencil and let whatever wanted to come out be drawn on paper. The little guy who came through told me his name is Hobodie Wort *(pronounced HA-ba-dee wart)* and he went on to say:

> *I have fun and dance on stones –*
> *Skip on water –*
> *Jump in the high grass.*
> *I love this world.*

I really felt it might be offensive to Hobodie to make him be the Fool. But he insisted and in the process he helped me understand the meaning a little better. As you can see, Hobodie is in a rather topsy-turvy position, appearing as if he might go head-first into the water next to the stone on

O The Fool

which he is dancing. Yet he seems to be perfectly happy, unafraid of the consequences if he were to tumble headlong into the water. Even so, he does seem to be completely in control of his actions.

Creating this card helped me to understand the pure happiness one can experience simply by doing what he feels is right, even if unexpected occurrences follow. One may go "out of his element" right into another that is completely different, but if he does it happily and fearlessly, then nothing can really go wrong for him. And like Hobodie, who loves to jump around so much, he can "bounce back" and start all over again.

The appearance of this card in a reading may indicate that, at present, someone's judgment may not be sound. Still, we must remain aware that we are here to experience the liberty and perhaps failure of our own free will. Preventing an individual from doing so only inhibits his personal growth. Sometimes we all need to take chances. If we go into things with a healthy, happy attitude, then we will have gained *something* – even if our original plans do not succeed. Nothing is lost by *trying*.

Reversed Meaning: *Carelessness. Negligence. Stupidity. Reckless behavior. Folly and indiscretion. Time to grow up and act responsibly.*

The Fool in a reversed position indicates carelessness, stupidity, and recklessly taking unnecessary risks – or not taking risks at all. Sometimes we need to take chances, but in a well-thought-out and responsible manner. Taking risks without considering the ramifications can lead to bad mistakes and possible destruction – be it of lives, property, or feelings. It is time to grow up and be reasonable. Reevaluate your potential actions and decisions, lest you or someone else get hurt by them.

I - The MAGICIAN

I The Magician

Meaning: *Intelligence. Power. Shrewdness. The ability or need to control and manipulate one's environment or surroundings.*

The Magician prepares to practice his arts in the dark of night. Balanced on a fallen tree, which he uses for an altar, are four items representing the elements in the suits of this deck – a sword, wand, ruby goblet, and crystal sphere. The goblet is red, the color of blood and life while the tip of his wand glows yellow, the color of illumination.

The landscape behind the Magician appears barren as a forest in winter, yet the fallen tree before him sprouts new foliage thanks to the magic worked by this most powerful sorcerer. The moon and stars symbolize the powers of the universe without whose help the Magician could not accomplish his great feats.

Perched on a tree behind the Magician is his familiar (an animal-shaped spirit that assists him) – a hawk, which has the ability to see things in broad perspective thus enabling it to ignore trivial details in its environment and zero in on its true target. This is an ability the Magician utilizes in order to achieve optimum results in the shortest amount of time possible. The Magician is a person who knows what he wants as well as the quickest way to achieve that goal.

The Magician wears an orange robe – the color of fire – to represent the great power he possesses and wields. He is powerful and confident – always sure of his actions and the reactions he hopes to cause in others. He can be an extremely wise and benevolent friend who is capable of doing anything for those he cares about. But woe be unto those who incur his wrath. The Magician is a powerful and deadly enemy who has the ability to destroy anything that hinders his plans.

The Magician himself should be a bit wary, because power is an awesome thing. The ability to use it is a gift not to be abused. Power used to help others will remain a steady force and increase in magnitude. Power used in an arrogant, selfish, and destructive manner will only get out of control and eventually dissipate, leaving its wielder helpless and alone.

The appearance of this card in a reading may indicate the presence of an individual with characteristics like the Magician's. It may also indicate that the querent himself has a need to control a situation, which he may easily do, but perhaps with adverse consequences. We all have power and it is not something to be taken lightly. We need to respect the abilities we are given and use them to help others rather than to cause harm.

Reversed Meaning: *Weakness of will. Discontent. Charlatan or impostor. Agitator. Manipulator. Liar. Petulant behavior. Misuse of power.*

The Magician in its reversed position indicates a weakness of will and lack of confidence that may be masked by a facade of arrogance. One's own discontent may cause him to become self-serving and manipulative, behaving in a petulant manner toward others. This card warns of the misuse of power for destructive ends. The ability to harm or control others does not make one superior.

The Magician reversed can prove to be a real agitator, stirring up emotions for his own amusement. His apparent prowess is a sham. This card is indicative of an impostor or charlatan who is trying to fool himself as well as others.

II The High Priestess

II - The HIGH PRIESTESS

Meaning: *Divine Wisdom. Enlightenment. Peace. Understanding or the need to understand the reasons things work the way they do.*

While Buffalo Calf Woman is a divine being who came to the Lakota Indians at a time when they greatly needed guidance. She bears the sacred pipe she presented to them with instructions that it must be smoked in a state of peace, with no negative thoughts, lest the usage of the pipe be profaned. The smoke of the pipe is a visual representation of the breath of mankind, swirling upward in prayer to the heavens. The greatest way to accomplish anything is through prayer – asking the forces of Nature and the Universe to aid us in whatever we need to accomplish.

We are all spirit beings – beings of light. We breathe light into ourselves each time we inhale, consequently breathing in the light/life force that surrounds us, making it a part of ourselves.

Conversely, each time we exhale, some of our own essence, our own mind, flows out on our breath to everything around us; therefore, it is important we be at peace, lest any negativity we feel be breathed out upon another. All of our actions – even the most minute – have profound impact on the entire Universe.

The tranquil expression on White Buffalo Calf Woman's face reminds us that we must be calm and at peace to commune well with others and to allow our most sincere prayers to come from the silence, stillness, and depths of our hearts. From that calm peacefulness comes wisdom, and with wisdom comes the realization that everything you need to know is already within yourself.

White Buffalo Calf Woman stands under a full moon in the dark of night between two trees, one black, the other white, to remind us of polar opposites and the fact that in order for us to recognize and respect Light, we must also experience Darkness. The "Seven Sisters" of the Pleiades grace the sky above her, emanating feminine energy and inspiring creativity, as well as a deep connection to the other side.

The appearance of this card in a reading may indicate a need to calm down and allow yourself to become more balanced and at peace. If it is easier to see things more clearly when we are calm, imagine how much clearer our *actions* are when we are at peace with ourselves and the world around us! The essence of the High Priestess is wisdom, understanding, and enlightenment – we gain these things by going into the stillness of our own hearts and listening to what the Powers of the Universe have to teach us. This card is a reminder that we are not alone – there are myriad Spirits all around, just waiting to help and teach us, and the best way to communicate with them is through prayer. Light some sage or incense in thankfulness, and watch the smoke take your prayers up to the heavens.

Reversed Meaning: *Superficial knowledge. Shallowness. Secrets revealed. Laziness. Difficulty accessing your intuitive feminine side. Misjudgment. Passion. Tartness.*

The High Priestess reversed may indicate a shallow person with only superficial knowledge and a tendency toward bubbly, gushing behavior. She may also represent a lazy person who has a penchant for practicing the darker side of spiritual manifestations; someone who experiences difficulty accessing her feminine side and intuition. Because the reversal indicates an effervescent personality, secrets may be revealed due to lack of judgment.

III - The EMPRESS

III The Empress

Meaning: *Mother. Fertility. Domestic Harmony – in society as well as the home.*

Titania is known as the Queen of the Fairies. Here she is depicted tending to one of the myriad flowers in her kingdom. She is the embodiment of femininity and grace, nurturing and loving all those around her.

Titania is dressed in white and adorned with flowers of Springtime – the season known for fertility and regeneration. She is the honest simplicity and beauty of motherhood, the kind and gentle woman all go to in their time of need.

Titania is also joint ruler of the Kingdom of Faery. As such, she is a powerful figure and one who commands respect and authority. The denizens of Faery adore Titania because of her kind and loving ways. They gladly appear whenever she holds court, simply to be in her genial presence. She knows how to make her world run smoothly. If you but pay attention to her gentle ways, then you too can make your own world run just as smoothly.

The appearance of the Empress in a reading may indicate a pregnancy. It also makes reference to domestic tranquility or the need for such and the ability to turn a house into a home through loving attentiveness to decor, plants, pets, and family members. The Empress is queen of her domain and it is up to her to make certain things run smoothly, whether it be the day to day running of her household, helping a child with his school project, or hostessing a banquet. The Empress can handle anything that comes her way.

This card may symbolize the querent's own mother or perhaps a need to "mother" the world. That is not a bad thing as nurturing is the kindest gift one can give. It teaches us about love and enables us to grow.

Reversed Meaning: *Vanity. Fickleness. Overindulgence. Seduction. Unloving nature. Infidelity. Lack of creativity. Infertility. Socially unacceptable behavior.*

A reversal of the Empress card implies the negative feminine traits of vanity and fickleness. It is indicative of a selfish and unloving nature that is prone to overindulgence and socially unacceptable behavior. Creative abilities may be stifled as a result of the infertility that is denoted by this reversal.

Seduction may be used in a deceitful manner, simply to enhance one's own self-esteem, or perhaps for even darker purposes. A woman may not be above entrapping a man by becoming pregnant or at least making the object of her desire believe that she is with child.

The Empress reversed warns of infertility and perhaps even the loss of a child through abortion, miscarriage, or problems during delivery. It may be time to reevaluate your thoughts about what a woman is or should be. Before you can take care of others, you need to be capable of tending to your own self.

IV - The EMPEROR

IV The Emperor

Meaning: *Father. Regenerative forces. Worldly protection. Responsibility. Willpower. Law. Intellect. Dominance. Stability.*

Oberon is known as the King of the Fairies. He is the counterpart to Titania and as such, he is the father-figure and protector of all his subjects. Like Titania, he also commands respect and is revered by all. When the denizens of Faery have a problem, they look to the Emperor for help, just as one would look to his own father.

Where the Empress acts through the heart, the Emperor uses intellect to pursue any course of deliberation or action. He is a kindly dictator, a man who has earned his status through many years of experience and thoughtful, calculated actions that have always worked to the benefit of those around him.

Oberon is depicted holding a dead tree branch, with autumn leaves in his hair. He rules the waning seasons, just as Titania rules the waxing ones. Even though autumn is a time when much in Nature seems to pass away, Oberon is the regenerative force that sustains the environment through the cold winter months, allowing the natural world to be reborn in the spring with Titania's help.

The appearance of the Emperor in a reading may indicate a father-figure or father-to-be. It also speaks of the need to take responsibility for others and to realize that people look up to you and rely on you for support and guidance. You may need to look at how you fit into society and how you deal with the hierarchy that naturally exists within it. While one should always have love and respect for others, he should not be forced to give up his own power just to make others feel more important. The presence of this card may indicate that it is time to exert your authority and show your expertise to others, especially in the workplace.

Reversed Meaning: *Stubbornness. Opposition. Immaturity. Tyranny. Misuse of Power. Chauvinism. Weak character.*

A reversal of the Emperor card suggests the misuse of power, be it your own or that of someone you admire. As is the case in all readings, this card could make reference to another person in your life, but you need to be open to the awareness that it might just as easily be referring to *you*. Take a long look at yourself and make sure that you are not taking an overly dominant position in someone's life. We all need to be respected and given space to breathe, think, and move. Make sure you are not hindering the growth of another person by your own domineering actions and beliefs.

This card reversed indicates stubbornness and a general immaturity. Remember that people do not tend to respect someone they feel acts like a child. A weak character shows itself quickly, and respect for that person flies out the window, regardless of his apparent status. True character is expressed by a willingness to listen to others and deal fairly and rationally with them.

V - The HIEROPHANT

V. The Hierophant

Meaning: *Divine Will. Interpretation of the Law of God in terms of personal and social behavior. Unity. Alliance. Duty. Instruction.*

This card is actually representative of a dream I had:

A peasant woman stood atop a knoll and struck the ground rather forcefully with her staff.

My own thoughts pervaded the dream and I said, "She should not have hit the Earth like that – it's mean."

At that moment in my dream, a large, leather bound, ancient tome appeared and opened to a page where I beheld the writing:

> *She did it without malice.*
> *She did it with intent.*
> *She knew what she was doing.*

I felt rather humbled at that point, especially when my dream continued. The woman still stood smiling upon the knoll which I realized was a fairy mound because several dwarves, elves, and other fairies had come out of the mound and started cavorting all around. The woman – who I later came to realize must have represented myself – was summoning the fairies out of the mound and they were all quite happy about it.

I always knew that each of us possesses powers that others have deemed "super-natural." That is, powers which are outside the realm of (understood) natural phenomena. Many individuals have been afraid to utilize those powers because of the fear and misunderstanding of the people around us. Society ingrained certain beliefs in each of us and quite often those beliefs are hard to get past, especially if one is afraid of offending or hurting loved ones in the process. Yet there comes a time when we each must stand up for our beliefs and religious preferences, regardless of how society feels about it.

This card symbolizes religious authority and the knowledge of secret mysteries as well as the ability to exert authority over others. You must choose your own path in life and decide how to relate to people who do not share your beliefs. You have the power to teach others, but you should always keep your mind open to what others are able to teach *you*, as well. This card may indicate a union or alliance of some sort along with the duties and responsibilities inherent in a blending of personal beliefs and lifestyles.

Reversed Meaning: *Rigid morality. Inflexibility. Superstition. Improper conduct. Unwise unions. Power derived through selfish pursuits.*

This card carries the warning that you must be careful of pushing your views onto others or forcing them to do things that go against their beliefs. Remember – other people's principles are as valid to them as yours are to you. The world is a vast place, full of different environments and people. No one is above anyone else. Our primary goals in life should be to improve our behavior and become more connected to the spiritual world and one another.

The Hierophant reversed also advises against unwise unions, be they the blending of institutions, beliefs, or specific individuals. We must remain firm in our own beliefs, while staying open-minded to others.

VI The Lovers

VI - The LOVERS

Meaning: *Romance. Temptation. Desires. Choosing between two loves – possibly making the wrong choice and hurting someone in the process.*

This card depicts the beautifully haunting and sad story of Undine. She was a water nymph who became human and fell in love, yet forfeited her life when the man she loved chose another over her.

Undine is shown desperately grasping the hand of her lover, even as she begins to return to the waters from which she sprang. The man and his new love look on at Undine, perhaps pityingly, knowing that their true love has cost the life of an innocent spirit. Yet rays shine down on Undine, symbolic of her impending return to the spirit world and a new life filled with renewed hope.

A facet of this card is the fact that we often try to seek out that which is strange and magical to us, thinking that it will be what we have always longed for, only to later discover we were actually better off with what we were more accustomed to. This card prompts us to think twice before we are tempted to give up what we have in favor of what may simply be an illusory dream.

This card also warns us that changing ourselves simply to meet someone else's expectations will not necessarily gain us the object of our heart's desire. The mere fact that you feel a need to change should show that what you are hoping for is not necessarily what is best for you. None of us is perfect. There is always room for improvement but still, we should be accepted for *who we are*.

The Lovers card also shows us that even if we are the ones who are cast aside in a relationship, or things do not work out as we plan in general, it is not truly the end of our lives. Better things are always waiting for us even though it may not appear so at the time.

Reversed Meaning: *Doubts. Lack of trust. Seduction. Temptation. Improper behavior. Unfaithfulness. Fear of being alone.*

The Lovers card reversed may imply doubts and distrust in a current relationship. It may also suggest that one is being drawn away from another by something seductive, be it a person or something in the nature of a drug, alcohol, or food addiction.

The appearance of this card in a reading may indicate that the querent or someone she cares about is "looking for greener pastures." Be aware that the grass is not always greener on the other side of the fence and that more than one person may be hurt by a careless desire to have something that only *appears* to be better.

One should also bear in mind that human beings cannot help who they are attracted to, and that the loss of someone who no longer loves you is *not* the end of the world. Quite often, we only search for love out of fear that we will be alone, but we must remember that we are *never* really alone – that is simply a state of mind. Before you seek the love of others, make sure that you love and are quite happy with your *self*. Only then will you truly be able to understand how to love another.

29

VII - The CHARIOT

VII The Chariot

Meaning: *Triumph. Success. Conquest. Overcoming obstacles. Anger. Pride. Travel.*

The Chariot card depicts a boggle (a mischievous elf or goblin) who has managed to harness two powerful *Cu Sith (pronounced ku shee)*, or fairy dogs, to a wagon which is more than likely stolen from an unsuspecting farmer. The wagon hurtles across a stone bridge almost out of control, as the two fairy dogs begin to run in opposite directions in an attempt to free themselves of their harnesses. The black and white dogs symbolize opposites and the balance necessary to achieve success in any endeavor. Although fairy dogs typically appear as large, imposing black hounds, white dogs have also been known to appear to humans. Normally, people perceive these creatures as omens of death, but from personal experience, I know they also can help save lives.

The boggle seems to be somewhat in control of the cart for the moment, but if the scenario illustrated in this card plays out, the fairy dogs will more than likely break their bonds and the cart will either crash or leave the boggle stranded. Much of the outcome depends upon the actions of the boggle and how he continues to treat the fairy dogs.

The appearance of this card in a reading shows that you are holding the reins to a situation that will end in success, provided you manage to maintain control and balance. Anger, pride, or simply the desire to show others you are in charge and can handle the situation may be the driving forces behind your triumph, but you must remain aware that others are helping you accomplish your goal and you should treat them kindly and with fairness.

This card represents a powerful person with a responsible nature. Strong emotions are indicated by this card, but if they are kept under control, obstacles will be overcome and victory will be achieved through hard work. This is a time for journeys and your travels will be in comfort.

Reversed Meaning: *Disputes. Competition. Failure. Accidents. Bad news.*

The Chariot card reversed warns of conflict and failure due to arrogance. This card is the epitome of the old adage, *pride goeth before a fall.* You must make certain that your goals are honorable and just before you coerce others to help you achieve them. It is bad enough if your own plans fail. It is far worse if you take down others with you.

You need to maintain a level head and a bit of humility, especially when you are the one holding the reins, because arrogance may cause carelessness. There is nothing wrong with forging ahead to achieve your objectives, but you need to be careful of using or hurting others in the process.

Part of the symbolism of this card is the harnessing of opposites and, because of that, you must be aware that there is always room for conflict. Whenever opposing forces are compelled to act side by side, there will be competition and disputes. Try to bear in mind that just as others may not always be wrong, *you* also may not always be right.

Because of the sheer force of this card, a reversal may indicate bad news or accidents to come. Slow down!

VIII - STRENGTH

VIII Strength

Meaning: *Triumph. Greatness. Overcoming obstacles. Spiritual strength and force of will. Victory in the face of overwhelming odds.*

A unicorn gracefully but powerfully gallops through water, spraying droplets in its wake as it races toward its goal. The unicorn has long been a symbol of purity and strength, showing itself only to those who are pure of heart and action. Fairies are some of the fortunate beings who are readily allowed contact with these magnificent creatures and the unicorn can serve as a bridge between our world and theirs.

Water is symbolic of the spirit realm and this unicorn forges unhesitatingly through it. Is it reentering the land of Faery or is it coming into our third dimension to show its inhabitants the power that is to be derived from its example of strength, grace, and spirituality?

I have been fortunate to witness the beauty, power, and love of unicorns in my dreams. I must say that in their presence I feel the utmost serenity and contentment. One of my dreams portrayed a ghostly, elegant herd of unicorns, hauntingly bathed in blue and white light as they galloped across the lawn behind my home. The sheer magnificence of their exquisite beauty and power thankfully remains emblazoned on my mind. Other dreams have graced me with the friendship of a baby unicorn who wants nothing more than to play in the water or be held by me. He has shown me symbolically how important it is to embrace your spiritualism, and to revel in it, but not to take yourself so seriously that you feel spiritually superior to others.

Where the Chariot signifies power over others, the Strength card symbolizes power from within. Inner powers are driven primarily by instinct and will "kick in" when you need them most. Whether you realize it or not, your spiritual strength is what you rely on and defer to when the going gets rough. It is what drives you and provides you the fortitude to continue.

The appearance of this card in a reading indicates that strength of will, strength of purpose, and spiritual strength are necessary to overcome any obstacles on one's path. As long as one realizes that the spirit is eternal, then there is nothing to fear in this physical world.

Reversed Meaning: *Weakness. Succumbing to temptation. The power of governments and kingdoms. Tyranny.*

The Strength card reversed signifies weakness and giving in to temptation. It is indicative of the often questionable power wielded by governments and those in authority. You must remember that *you* are an individual with your own beliefs and ideals and you should not succumb to others simply to reinforce *their* powers.

A reversal of this card may indicate that you are becoming aware of your own magical power and the ability to enchant others. Make sure you use your gifts in a beneficial, rather than a malevolent or immoral way.

IX The Hermit

IX - The HERMIT

Meaning: *Wisdom. Solitude. Open-mindedness. Desire to learn. Seeking the Truth. Looking within.*

A solitary fairy kneels before the cave in which she resides, holding the light of truth in her hand. She is prepared to share this truth with those who are wise enough to behold it. An owl, the symbol of wisdom, sits beside her.

The solitude of the cave allows the quiet and peace of mind necessary to explore the depths of one's soul, while the darkness serves to enhance the beautiful illumination brought by wisdom. The hermit may live alone, but with the knowledge and glow of truth surrounding her, she is never lonely.

The Hermit card signifies wisdom and the desire to learn. In order to truly obtain the understanding we seek, we should keep our minds and our hearts open to whatever truths present themselves, regardless of how disquieting they may be. In the calm solitude of our being, we can open ourselves to the mysteries of the universe and reflect on them with the attention and respect they deserve. Bear in mind that divine guidance can and will lead you to amazing discoveries about yourself and the world around you if you are willing to humble yourself and truly listen. The Hermit may indicate a need to separate oneself from the world for a time, simply to reconnect with the Universe. The hustle and bustle of our modern society quite often does not allow for "down time." We all need to sit back, relax, and do some introspective thinking. Everything we need to know is already inside our own selves.

Reversed Meaning: *Reclusiveness. Timidity. Loneliness. Unsocial behavior. Concealment. Fear.*

A reversal of the Hermit card may indicate that one has too much of a reclusive nature, either stemming from timidity or perhaps a general disdain for society. While we all need time to ourselves, we also need the companionship of others, if for no other reason than to help us keep our feet firmly rooted to the ground and realize that we were put on this earth to experience life – which includes other people and their beliefs.

The Hermit reversed may signify that you or someone else have something you are trying to hide. Fear causes us to shut ourselves off from outside influences that we feel may harm us. But we need to be aware that there are also others outside who may have exactly what we need to help us. Shutting yourself off from the world does nothing to enlighten you – it only causes loneliness.

This card is dedicated to the precious little owl who sat in the pouring rain not ten feet away from me one lonesome night when I felt I had nothing. There is always *something* with us, whether we are fortunate enough to realize it or not.

X The Wheel of Fortune

X - The WHEEL OF FORTUNE

Meaning: *Fate. Fortune. Good luck. Prosperity. Happiness. Ups and downs in life.*

I chose a fairy ring to represent the Wheel of Fortune, since it is such an important part of fairy lore. Fairies are fickle by nature, one moment happy to help someone and the next moment angered beyond reasoning at the smallest offense. It is totally up to their discretion whom they wish to help or harm. The fairy ring is a prime example of that.

People were continually warned to beware of fairy rings, especially at night, as fairies were wont to lure unsuspecting travelers into the midst of their revels, often forcing the hapless stranger to dance himself to death before the morning dawned. Once a person walked into a fairy ring, there was no escape, unless he happened to have a friend outside the ring, ready to pull him to safety.

If befriended by the fairies, one's fate could change in an instant. They could bestow wealth, happiness, and general good fortune on those they admired. But woe be unto those who incurred the fairies' wrath – ill-fortune, unhappiness, and death were the likely outcomes. Some particular types of fairies are seen as being inherently evil. Most fairies, however, are simply mischievous, often playing tricks on unsuspecting humans. These tricks are usually well-deserved lessons in disguise. The fairies cannot abide lazy or mean people and the pranks devised by fairies are a means of making the offender aware of what he has done wrong. By the same token, fairies delight in giving a good person whatever riches they feel he deserves.

So the Fairy Ring, in this way, becomes a sort of "wheel of fortune" – what appears to be a terrible stroke of bad luck is, in fact, retribution for a wrong committed or a "testing by fire" to see if one is worthy of something better to come. And then again, sometimes a wealth of good may come to one for no apparent reason. The fickle nature of Faery mirrors the fickle nature of Fate.

The appearance of this card in a reading signifies that the Wheel of Fortune is turning, and that good things are coming your way. Life is full of ups and downs but now is a time of happiness and good luck.

Reversed Meaning: *Bad luck. Misfortune. Excess. Fall from power.*

The Wheel of Fortune reversed indicates that your luck is changing – probably for the worse. You may have had an overabundance of good fortune, perhaps unmerited, and now the wheel is turning to balance itself.

Problems you may now face will be tests of your fortitude and integrity. Just as the fairies reward the good and bad they see in people, so does society. If your endeavors are upstanding, then things will likely change for the better in short time. If you are being less than honest and kind, then expect vengeance from the fates.

XI - JUSTICE

XI Justice

Meaning: *Justice. Balance. Honesty. Open-mindedness. Seeing both sides of an issue.*

Beautiful Justice sits on her throne, ready to serve those who seek her assistance. She balances scales on her wand, although magic is not necessary to see the truth. Her right hand rests on a sword, ready to cut through the ignorance of unbalanced minds. She wears green, the color of growth, which symbolizes the fact that those of us who make a conscious effort to be fair and just will mature spiritually while those who do not will remain in their unbalanced state until they see the wisdom of Justice.

The appearance of this card in a reading indicates that it is time to face facts and be held accountable for your actions. You may be involved in a law suit or a hearing of some sort, but as long as you are truthful and willing to accept responsibility for your actions, things will go well for you.

You may feel that you are being judged or treated unfairly in a situation, but you need to ask yourself if your motives are all totally above-board. If you are being honest, upstanding, and have nothing to hide, you have nothing to fear.

Justice is balanced and fair. It does not choose sides. It chooses Truth. Justice entails the ability to retain an open mind and use wisdom to cut through to the heart of a matter.

This card denotes an imperative to be honorable in one's dealings. If we wish to be treated fairly, then we must do no less for others.

Reversed Meaning: *Codified Law. Inequality. Bias. Injustice or abuse of the legal system. False accusations. Dishonesty.*

The Justice card reversed indicates the possibility of *Injustice*, due to bias, prejudice, or a simple unwillingness to truly listen and weigh an issue fairly. Those in power are fully capable of using their influence against more helpless individuals.

False accusations may be flying right now, and you may find yourself in an embarrassing situation. Even if you have done nothing wrong, it may be hard to prove your case to others. You need to remain balanced and truthful. Emotional outbursts could be very damaging, regardless of how right you may feel you are. Have the courage to stand your ground and prove you are the better person.

Dishonesty may be the crux of your problems – either someone is being untruthful with you, or you may be acting less than honorable yourself. In the end, Truth will show itself and Justice will be served. Make sure you have no reason to fear either one of them.

Another aspect of this card reminds us to make sure that we are not sitting in judgment of someone else. We may not always agree with the lifestyles or beliefs of others, but it is ultimately not up to us to judge anyone besides our own selves. Our society invented courts and the justice system to deal with crimes that truly harm innocent individuals, but when others are merely living their lives in a way that doesn't coincide with what society feels is right, that does not necessarily make them wrong.

Remember the old adage:

Judge not, lest you be judged.

XII The Hanged One

XII - The HANGED ONE

Meaning: *Spiritual growth. Attainment of wisdom. Surrender to a higher power. Learning to trust the power within.*

In this card, a young woman hangs from the branch of a tree at dusk while gathering fairies and elves witness the event. A stool from the woman's home lies kicked aside, and although she appears to struggle with the rope around her neck, she is actually only testing the full extent of her own powers, fully confident that she will be able to free herself. The denizens of Faery, however, are ready to come to her aid should she need it.

The woman's solitary lifestyle and surroundings are reminiscent of the free, country-dwelling lives led by so many who were wrongly accused of witchcraft centuries ago. Perhaps to some degree, she wishes to experience what those poor, misunderstood individuals went through simply because they chose to lead lives off the beaten path. At any rate, she has no fear of death, since it is merely another experience necessary for the growth of one's soul. Being a child of nature, she is fully aware of the countless spiritual allies surrounding her, ready to aid her in whatever way possible.

The woman attempts her feat at twilight – the time when the physical world begins to merge with that of Faery. It is a time of change that allows one to behold the threshold of the spirit realm, just as the moment of death opens the gate to that same kingdom. The woman has opened herself up to the higher realms and has surrendered her will to a higher power, well aware that no matter what happens she will be protected.

The appearance of this card in a reading signifies change and the need to surrender oneself to the higher powers. Some sacrifice may need to be made, but only by letting go of self and seeking true wisdom will our souls be able to grow and attain their proper place in the universe. Trust in your own abilities, but be aware that there are other forces in the universe that are even more powerful, ready to love and attend you in any way they can.

Reversed Meaning: *Selfishness. Inability or unwillingness to follow through on something – be it a promise, a creative idea, or the intention to change things.*

The Hanged One reversed indicates rather selfish desires. Apparent sacrifices made publicly are merely for show, simply to allow oneself to be regarded as a martyr. You may feel tied down or in limbo at this time, and the best way to rectify the situation is by *action*. Any movement is preferable to waiting indefinitely for something to happen.

Promises made are unlikely to be kept. It is easy to vow to change things or to do good deeds when one feels imperiled, but it takes much more fortitude to actually follow through with such oaths after the danger has passed. If you do not really mean something, do not promise it – after all, a man is only as good as his word. Even if you have only made a promise to yourself, it is best to try to keep it – if nothing else, it will serve to strengthen faith in your own resolve and sense of self.

XIII Death

XIII - DEATH

Meaning: *Change. Rebirth. Renewal. Transformation.*

A banshee (in Gaelic folklore, a female spirit that warns of an impending death) wails as thunderbolts strike from out of a raging storm. A solitary light shines in the ancestral home of the family to which she has attached herself while bolts of lightning buffet the castle walls. The banshee heralds change for the family of this ancient castle – the passing of one of the clan's lineage to a better realm.

This card, however, does not in fact signify actual death, but merely Transformation. Even an event so seemingly terrible as the loss of a loved one is actually a new beginning for that entity. Everything in life transforms – that is how we grow and progress. Sometimes changes are very uncomfortable but when looked upon with hindsight, we are usually able to see the beneficial effects created by the transformations in our lives.

Just like the lightning in the picture, change can often strike us like a bolt out of the blue, startling us, and perhaps frightening us for a short period of time. But like the solitary light glowing within the castle walls, we know there will always be a light at the end of the tunnel – a hope upon which our hearts may rest.

Changes allow us to start anew – think of something as simple as changing hair color. Changes also give us the chance to act a bit differently – hopefully, in a more mature and wise manner than before we experienced something outside the realm of our day-to-day existence. Even when we do not immediately appreciate change, it ultimately helps with our development. Change should be glorified, not feared, because it is what keeps life from becoming stagnant.

The appearance of this card in a reading signifies change to come, although not necessarily of a bad sort. Things may happen in a way you do not expect, but just flow – and grow – with the tide. This could be the beginning of a whole new life for you!

Reversed Meaning: *Stagnation. Disillusionment. Narrow escape from death or accident.*

While the Death card does not necessarily signify a death, the reversal of this card may indicate a narrow escape from death or accident. Just remember that when bad things happen, it is usually to cause us to pause and think about where we are headed in life. The Death card may simply indicate that you are unsatisfied with your life at the moment. When our lives become stagnant, we need to make changes of some sort to keep progressing. But if this card is reversed, you may be afraid to allow change into your life at this time.

You may be disillusioned with the world, but in reality, it all boils down to how you feel about your *self*. It may be time to make over yourself – your attitude, your appearance, your job, or your home life. There are so many little changes we are all capable of making that could brighten up our lives. You need not make a total transformation – sometimes, just getting a new outfit or smiling when you feel like frowning are enough to make you feel the difference.

XIV - TEMPERANCE

XIV Temperance

Meaning: *Peace. Harmony. Balance. Control. Healing. Sustaining life.*

A deva draws moisture from the night air to create the dewdrops that bathe and nourish the earth, aiding the plants in their growth. Her majestic, serene presence is an essential element in the life cycles of all the vegetation in her domain. To the verdure of her surroundings, she is the Queen of the Night – the loving and nurturing Mother whose succor sustains all within her realm. After I created this card, I tried to "connect" with a deva, one of the many territorial spirits that care for the outside world. My thoughts drifted along, and my mind unconsciously wandered to how wonderful it would be to exist as a deva with the purpose of creating life. At that moment, I was gently chided by an outside voice poignantly saying, "No. *Sustaining* life." Those three words helped me realize the true nature of this card.

While Temperance most definitely involves balance, control, peace and harmony, it is the focusing of these elements toward the purpose of *sustaining* life that makes this particular card of such great importance. If we each act in such a selfless, loving, and giving manner – as the devas do to maintain the health and further the growth of the natural world – then our own world will be that much better. We would greatly benefit our selves not only by practicing these attitudes, but by sharing them with others.

Just as the old adage says, "What goes around comes around." When we give thoughtfully and lovingly to the world, it will give back to us in kind – that is balance.

The appearance of this card in a reading indicates that balance is needed. You or someone you know needs to act with peace and harmony so that things naturally fall into their correct places. This may involve the blending of separate ideas or beliefs, and a certain degree of give and take is necessary. Remember that your actions can be guided with the idea of sustaining life and making it better instead of detracting from it.

Reversed Meaning: *Discord. Lack of Balance. Mood swings. Illness.*

A reversal of the Temperance card indicates a great need to exercise control and balance. This may be due to a disagreement with another person or perhaps it is purely an internal conflict. Moods swings are likely and may even be caused by a chemical imbalance that needs to be checked. The appearance of this card in a reading could be indicative of a serious illness that requires not only professional assistance, but the willingness to do whatever is required to correct the disorder. It is imperative to remain calm and allow serenity to flow into your life and soothe whatever is causing you distress. Whatever you put out, be it total negativity or a positive attitude, is what you will receive in turn.

XV - The DEVIL

XV The Devil

Meaning: *Pride. Fear. Ignorance. Selfishness. Choosing the Material over the Spiritual.*

A person rests his head against one of the two huge boulders that block his path. He is caught, quite literally, between a rock and a hard place as lightning bolts crash behind him. Life has become unbearable to him and he cannot even bring himself to look at his own reflection in the waters before him.

I personally do not believe in the devil. I do believe that evil spirits exist, but I also believe that each of us has the capacity for evil as well as good. I have long felt that one of the greatest problems with humankind is its penchant for creating a scapegoat such as the devil when something does not go according to plan. It is much easier to child-ishly create and blame an entity that people are willing to acknowledge as the epitome of evil rather than to admit our own wrongdoing.

We were all created with *free will* and it is up to each of us as individuals to do the right thing. The best choice is to accept responsibility for our own actions rather than to lay blame on someone or something else. We all act of our own volition whether we choose to admit that fact or not. Facing up to one's own actions is a sign of growth – unfortunately, there are not very many spiritually mature individuals in the world.

People also tend to blame society's ills on the devil being loose in the world. I have news for them – there are countless individuals who choose actions based on selfishness or fear. Why blame a made-up entity, like a devil, when there are plenty of people out there responsible for the shape the world is in today? If everyone held himself accountable for his own actions rather than laying the blame elsewhere, we might be able to pick up the pieces of the world we are destroying and make something better of it.

The appearance of this card in a reading indicates that material concerns are taking precedence over spiritual ones. Fear and ignorance may prevent you from seeing the truth behind an issue. Pride and selfishness need to be released so that you can look at the situation from a more unbiased position and make sure that you are not actually part of the problem. Do not be so quick to lay blame on others.

We all need to accept responsibility for our own actions.

Reversed Meaning: *Weakness. Bondage. Lust. Spiritual advancement. Virtue. Morality.*

The Devil card reversed can represent extremes in behavior. One may feel the very negative impact of being unable to escape bondage to someone or something. The querent needs to realize that his own free will is enough to gain freedom from such a seemingly hopeless situation. Just because temptation presents itself does not mean we have to follow.

On the other hand, a reversal of the Devil card may indicate that someone is or has become more virtuous and concerned with maintaining an upright lifestyle. This may also represent the attitude of someone who has turned his life around but achieved the adverse effect of self-righteous fanaticism that makes him refuse to admit that he has ever done anything wrong in his life.

XVI - The TOWER

XVI The Tower

Meaning: *Destruction. Upheaval of one's accustomed way of life. Enlightenment in the wake of sudden catastrophe.*

Animals and fairies hurriedly scatter for safety as the tree in which they reside is suddenly struck by lightning. These creatures comfort one another as they quietly watch the destruction of their home. Eventually, they will have to seek out new dwellings, but for now they are held in thrall by the awesome power of the Thunder-Beings responsible for the devastation of their abode.

I once pondered the reason trees are struck by lightning, and the following was imparted to me.

When Thunder-Beings strike a tree, one should not mourn for it, because it was *chosen*, like a sacrifice. It is much like when sage or sweetgrass are ignited in ceremonies. One uses them to purify – to inhale the aroma – gaining peace and spiritual strength through the smoke that pours out of the plant as its very essence rises back to the heavens. Just as we would have no compunction about lighting a small twig of sage, so the trees are in relation to the vastness of the Thunder-Beings and their universe.

In this card, the tree has gracefully given up its physical existence to honor the forces of nature from whence it sprang. The denizens of the tree bear witness to its selfless gift to the universe. While their erstwhile home is now destroyed, they at least survive to find a new one.

Natural disasters are a fact of life. They throw our lives into terrible upheaval, but they are representative of change. While change can be quite painful at times, it happens so that we may learn by experience and grow in spirit. A side effect of disasters – natural or otherwise – is the coming together of individuals who experience them. Sometimes it takes a catastrophe to bring out the qualities of caring and selflessness that human beings naturally posses but do not often impart.

The appearance of this card in a reading may indicate upheaval in one's life – unexpected, and perhaps devastating occurrences that seem to be of disastrous proportions to the individual. Take heart, however, in the awareness that new knowledge and a new outlook may be gained from the loss. This card may also be indicative of a need to release old patterns of thought or existence, so that a new perspective may be gained in one's life.

Reversed Meaning: *Disaster narrowly averted. Inner turmoil. Unwillingness to face a problem. Unexpected change.*

A reversal of the Tower card may indicate that you have narrowly avoided a disaster or accident. It could also indicate that a situation is about to reach its breaking point, simply because you refuse to recognize the import of an ongoing problem. Change may occur quite suddenly – you need to acknowledge what has happened, adapt and move on.

XVII - The STAR

XVII The Star

Meaning: *Hope. Serenity. Health – mental, physical, and spiritual. Inspiration. Divine guidance. Loving kindness. Oneness with the universe.*

Calm majesty exudes from the Spirit of the Star that gazes down upon the megalithic Stonehenge, which is an ancient calendar based upon the celestial observations of mankind's ancestors. Astrology and astronomy are but two of the gifts imparted to mankind by the celestial sphere of the Universe – gifts that have assisted mankind for millennia. Where would primitive farmers have been without knowledge of the cycles of the moon and stars, and how many major events in the world's history were planned according to the layout of the stars on any given day?

Although modern man acknowledges the import of astronomy insofar as science is concerned, he nevertheless has a tendency to laugh off belief in astrology. Of course, that is his misfortune, since there is a wealth of knowledge to be gleaned from the study of the stars.

Everything in the Universe – including celestial objects – has Spirit and a purpose for existence. Our daily interactions with one another have an impact on *everything* that occurs on our home planet. Everything that happens on Earth has a bearing on other celestial objects. Everything in the Universe has an integral relationship, and those interactions have a direct bearing upon each of us as individuals. The study of the stars enlightens us to our relationships with one another, as well as to the rest of the Universe. It also helps put in perspective how minuscule we as human beings are in the vastness of the Universe we inhabit. Still, I believe we are all Spirit, and all a part of the One Great Spirit that is the Center of the Universe and of our very Being.

The Star signifies the essence and light of our Being. Our spirits are like tiny points of light in the Universe, interacting in regulated times and places in the Cosmos, having a direct bearing upon everyone and everything we touch throughout our existence. As beings of Spirit, we *are* energy and light. As such, we are healthy and lively souls, moving at our own pace and acquiring the experience and knowledge we need to progress. The Star also expresses the hope we all carry for our pure enlightenment – the ultimate knowledge of our place in the Universe, and the wisdom to understand that we are part of a greater Whole.

The appearance of the Star in a reading signifies hope, health, and enlightenment. One should be aware of his/her relationship to everyone and everything else in the universe and that our very existence plays upon the lives of all surrounding us. Time heals all wounds and we never need fear, for we are watched over by the stars in their patient and endless march throughout time and space.

Reversed Meaning: *Lack of hope. Self-centeredness, causing either arrogant behavior or low self-esteem. Need to connect with Nature and the Universe as a Whole.*

The Star reversed may indicate a general feeling of hopelessness. Ego causes separation and can lead to feelings of either inadequacy or superiority. We must realize that we are all part of a much greater Whole, and accept the significance of ourselves from that perspective, rather than from the shallow viewpoint of society.

XVIII - The MOON

XVIII The Moon

Meaning: *Illusion. Deception. False hope. Dreams. Latent psychic powers.*

Two *Wilis (pronounced WILL-eez)* gaze mournfully at the full moon, lost in their illusions of love and hope. The *Wilis* were the spirits of young women, jilted in their love and departed from this life before they could exercise new hopes for a devoted relationship. Unfortunately, these spirits took a downward path and molded their existence merely to trap unwary men wandering the forests of the night, forcing them to dance to their deaths before the next dawn. In this way, the *Wilis* felt vindicated for their own past misfortunes.

A great moral lesson is to be learned from the *Wilis*. These hapless women allowed the veil of illusion to envelop their lives, hoping for more than a mere mortal man could give them. When they were disappointed and heartbroken, rather than wait for time to heal their wounds and give them hope for better future circumstances, they opted to end their lives, totally giving up on hope. Yet their spirits lived on in a realm of darkness, lying in wait to harm others as badly as they themselves were hurt. Their vengeance brought them no comfort, however – only an eternity of sorrow and loneliness.

The *Wilis* lived in a world of illusion and dreams. It must be remembered that Illusion and Hope are two different entities. Illusion is a veil that blankets our perceptions and clouds our judgment. Hope is the clarity within our souls that keeps us going, even when Illusion makes life seem unbearable. Dreams give us hope, but we must remember that *consciousness* is the world we live in day after day, so we need to be aware of what is "real" and deal with it in the healthiest way possible.

The appearance of this card in a reading indicates that you should be wary of illusion in your own life. Do not let yourself be blinded by how you *want* things to be. It is far easier in the long run to face things and deal with them head-on, even if it will mean temporary unhappiness. Change is a common theme of life – quite often it may seem for the worse but ultimately it is always for the better, as every experience in one's life is a lesson needed by the soul. Nothing in life is permanent, and your dissatisfaction with an event could easily wear off in a very short amount of time if you will hold on to hope and keep an open mind.

The Moon also indicates psychic abilities, so when you feel lost and alone, try tuning in to your own awareness and realize what a powerful person you really are.

Reversed Meaning: *Hidden things come to light. Tranquility. Willpower.*

A reversal of the Moon card indicates things are not as crazy as they may seem. Ideas or situations you thought implausible could prove to be very real as new facts arise. But it will take calmness and willingness on your part to make sure that you are trying to understand things clearly and without self-deception.

The moon is a powerful gravitational force that pulls on our thoughts and emotions. Allow the earth to keep you grounded when the elusive world of dreams brought on by the moon's power attempts to take hold of your psyche. Dreams only truly become active when they are grounded in reality.

XIX - The SUN

XIX The Sun

Meaning: *Happiness. Success. Health. Pleasure from the little things in life.*

Two little fairies sit atop a sunflower soaking in the last rays of daylight. Like sunflowers whose faces follow the path of the sun throughout the day, these fairies are wise enough to always follow the direction of light and happiness. If you have the ability to change your own position to make your life more contented, why not take advantage of that gift?

All too often, we get caught up in the daily rush of living and we forget to take time to appreciate all that the world offers us. Without the sun, life would cease to exist, yet every day it rises to provide warmth and energy to our planet. Our planet not only grants us a place to live, it provides all the necessities for sustaining life. Yet even more than that, the earth offers so many wonders that we take for granted – do you appreciate grass, trees, flowers, and a clear blue sky every day, or only when they are taken away from you? Do you value the bedrock that supports the earth you walk upon? Are you happy to see a rainstorm when it arrives, aware of the water it bestows on the earth, slaking our thirst and allowing us to survive?

It is so easy to ignore these blessings because we take them for granted, but we need to realize that they are just that – *granted* – and they can be taken from us at any time. How fortunate we are to have a Creator and nature spirits that constantly attend to such things so that we can carry on our busy lives and not even have to think about them. We are blessed in so many ways, and the best way to show our thanks is to be happy for all we have.

The appearance of this card in a reading signifies joy and health. We should be thankful for all the little pleasures in life that we receive on a daily basis. Because some things are so very simple, we tend not to take notice of them. This card reminds us not only to stop and smell the roses, but to take time to thank them for being there. In fact, we should take time to be thankful for our own gift of being.

Be grateful for the bounty of good fortune in your life and share your happiness with others. The world will love you for it!

Reversed Meaning: *Joy and accomplishment, but to a lesser degree. Overacting – pretending things are better than they really are. Refusing to see the good things in life.*

The Sun card reversed carries the same meaning as its upright position, but to a lesser degree. It may indicate that someone is actually feigning great happiness, when in reality a situation may not be quite so pleasant. Taken down another notch, a reversal of the Sun card may mean that someone refuses to acknowledge all the blessings life has offered that person.

Regardless of its position, the Sun card reminds us that we all have an enormous amount of things for which we should be grateful. It is quite easy to overlook our blessings when we are showered with so many all the time, but we do need to realize how fortunate we are and be thankful.

XX - JUDGMENT

XX Judgment

Meaning: *Renewal. Awakening. Spiritual transformation.*

A Phoenix rises from its own ashes onto a new life path. The flames of its rebirth represent the creative fires and movement of its own soul energy. The creature it has become, while it may appear different, is really the same entity it was before, albeit spiritually transformed to begin a new existence on a higher plane.

Judgment is ultimately based upon how we spiritually rise to our own ideals. We must face and answer to our *own* higher consciousness before we can progress to higher levels of being. One's conscience is a much stricter judge of character than anyone else could ever be. When we have truly met our own spiritual expectations, then we will be ripe for transition into higher realms, where we can further hone the growth of our souls.

Our society has made laws and grown so accustomed to judging others by them that we rarely take time to look at our own selves to make sure that we, too, are doing what is deemed right, not only by society but in our own hearts. Societal laws are not the only laws in the universe, nor are they always the correct ones. In fact, many of society's laws are made out of fear and misunderstanding

– two things that are definitely not conducive to spiritual growth. We need to be aware that it avails us nothing to sit in judgment on others. It is only ourselves that we are truly capable of judging.

The appearance of this card in a reading indicates an awakening for the individual. It is a time for renewal, for one to transform his or her nature for the better. Judgment is the ability to face our own thoughts and actions with a clear conscience, and then move onward and upward.

Reversed Meaning: *Bad judgment. Being judgmental. Inability to see things from a bigger and more spiritual perspective.*

A reversal of this card may mean that someone is judging you unfairly or perhaps that you are not using sound judgment in dealing with others. Because we are all brought up with certain beliefs, we often find it difficult to overcome preconceived notions of what is right and wrong – we tend to make snap judgments on the behavior of others, yet we never seem capable of looking at our own selves from such an unbiased viewpoint. The truth of the matter is that our Higher Consciousness knows better than we do what is correct, and we ultimately have to answer to it. We should concern ourselves more with that extremely important task, rather than feeling we need to decide what is best for the rest of the world.

Remember the old adage – *judge not, lest you be judged.* It is not our place to sit in judgment on anyone but our *own selves* – and that should be enough to keep anyone busy!

XXI - The WORLD

XXI The World

Meaning: *Fulfillment. Liberation. Success. Change for the better. Ability to lighten the lives of others.*

Gaia, or Mother Nature, walks blissfully through her domain of the world and its four seasons. She sees the totality of nature and all that must be accomplished in its own time throughout the year. Hers is the grace and beauty of a love that envelops not only the planet, but each person upon it who is allowed to partake of its wonders.

Like nature, our own souls are constantly in a state of change – from the spring-like newness of being through the calm summer-like serenity gained as we mature, to the mellow and heart-warming reminiscences of our autumn years to the wisdom and respite gained by the winter of our lives, as we await renewal in a new cycle of existence.

Simply living through the seasons of our lives and accepting them gracefully as they arrive is a blessing and source of fulfillment. Wishing for winter in spring denies you the beauty of a ripening summer and the nostalgia of the autumn. Desiring to turn back the hands of time from autumn or winter to earlier seasons will only make you lose sight of all the glory that surrounds you at the present moment. Every phase of Nature is a learning experience meant to be enjoyed in its entirety.

In its cyclic form, nature is a reflection of the universe. All things must come and go and then they will come and go again and again. Life never stops and all aspects of it should be absorbed and cherished. By living through all of life's changes, we can successfully complete things we came to this lovely world to accomplish.

The appearance of this card in a reading indicates success in all endeavors. Changes may come, just as they do in the natural world, but they will be for the better. Acceptance of life and its changes is a liberating force, one that helps you grow as you realize the sheer beauty of your existence and everything that surrounds you. Breathe in the essence of the world and let it draw you closer to the universe. Sharing your joy and peace with others will help lighten the planet and everything upon it.

Reversed Meaning: *Stagnation. Lack of foresight. Task left incomplete.*

The World card reversed carries much of its upright meaning – life is always in a constant state of change and we need to flow along with it, so that we may enjoy all it has to offer.

Reversed, this card may be indicative of stagnation or un-willingness to move forward. It could indicate longing for better times now past and an inability to look ahead to see what good things are yet to be.

This is a time to sit back and review what has been done, and what still needs to be accomplished. Quitting just be-cause one has reached a comfortable zone is not the best option. We are here to experience all of life, and to enjoy it as it comes.

Minor Arcana

Ace of Swords

Ace of Wands

Ace of Cups

 *Swords*

ACE OF SWORDS

Ace of Swords

Meaning: *Beginning of a conquest or victory. A fervent ability to both love and hate. Triumph. Possible birth of someone who will become a great leader.*

The Ace of Swords symbolizes the beginnings of a conquest or victory. The double-edged sword pictured here reflects the motivational forces of love and hate which reside in us all. Just as steel must be tempered to give strength to the sword, so must we learn to temper our emotions in order to achieve balance, strength of mind, and character.

You are ready to wage a battle, but to ensure victory, you must remain strong, straight, true, and to the point – just like a sword. You must focus your energies in a positive and controlled manner if you wish to cut through to the heart of a matter and rise to the top.

A sword inspires confidence and is a powerful weapon to possess and utilize if necessary. However, it is far easier to win people over through the influence of your own love and kindness than through any show of force. When you take the offensive, your opponent will automatically become *defensive*. Arm yourself with the power of love and good intentions and you will ultimately be the victor.

Since the Ace signifies beginnings, the appearance of this card in a reading may indicate the birth of someone who will become a great leader. The Ace implies the onset of a challenge, but it also suggests that you will be triumphant in the efforts you pursue.

Reversed Meaning: *Destructive, as well as constructive abilities. Competence to separate good from evil. Beware trying to use too much power to achieve your goal.*

While the Ace of Swords signifies the ability to separate good from evil, it also carries with it the *destructive* as well as *constructive* aspects of a two-edged sword. Beware your actions. Saying one thing and doing another is dishonorable. Not only is it confusing to others, it is damaging to your own character. This negative habit can express itself in so many ways – gossiping, lying, intending to go through with something and then backing out of it – all of these are cowardly aspects that do nothing to encourage the growth of your soul or inspire friendship and harmony.

A reversal of the Ace of Swords warns against using too much power to reach your goals. Nothing is really worth having if you must harm another in order to attain it. Selfishness and power add up to tyranny and no one appreciates a tyrant.

TWO OF SWORDS

2 Swords

Meaning: *Potential trouble ahead. Possible stalemate or temporary truce in a dispute. Indecision. Need for well-balanced emotions, diplomacy, and tact.*

One rainy day, I beheld the image of this creature in the bark of a favorite tree and felt compelled to draw it. Was he good, or possibly malevolent? I had no way of knowing but instinctually felt that he suited the essence of the Two of Swords.

Since the suit of swords represents aggression and the number two denotes balance, this card carries a reminder to be diplomatic and weigh both sides of an issue before taking action that may later be regretted. A perceived foe or threat may actually turn out to be a great ally or advantage. By the same token, automatically trusting a stranger may be a grave mistake. The Two of Swords reminds us to be wary.

Because the Two of Swords represents opposing forces, this card may indicate a stalemate or the inability to make a decision. Try to see both sides of a situation, but remain firm in your own resolve if you feel it is for the best.

When dealing with the unknown, stand back from the situation and evaluate all aspects of what lies before you. Do not automatically assume someone or something to be good or evil, safe or dangerous, friend or foe. Think of your own character and realize that nothing about us is simply black or white. Although we all possess the capacity for good and evil, love and hate, honesty and deceit, there are fine shades of gray throughout everything we think and do. Understand that all creatures possess the same capacities and use your own sense of balance to discern the truth. Remain open, but be cautious.

Reversed Meaning: *Betrayal. Treachery. Lies. Unbalanced emotions cloud your judgment.*

The Two of Swords reversed warns of betrayal, lies, and treachery. Although you perceive a situation to be a certain way, it may instead be the exact opposite of what you think.

A reversal of this card may signify that a person leans too far in one direction and could be unbalanced. It may also signify your own inability to see both sides of a situation, or a tendency to blindly follow your own way of thinking without even considering other options. Some of the worst problems in the world are caused by the one-sided beliefs and opinions of individuals who cannot understand ideas that run counter to their own. Matters run more smoothly when balance is maintained.

THREE OF SWORDS

3 Swords

Meaning: *Separation due to strife. Quarrels. Incompatibility. Upheaval in the family. Possible political conflict. Lovers separated by war or misfortune.*

Since Medieval times, dragons have been notorious for hoarding and carefully guarding treasures. The rationale behind these myths, however, may carry a much deeper significance. Legends of dragons protecting treasure can be traced back to the ancient Greeks. The goddess Hera had a dragon that guarded a tree of golden apples which contained the secrets and knowledge of immortality. Therefore, the treasure so fiercely protected by dragons may actually be knowledge long hidden from mankind. Dragons have thick skin and may be able to handle the truth (i.e., forbidden knowledge) better than a mere mortal.

This card depicts a dragon ferociously guarding its treasure trove, driving its mate from their lair in a fit of greed. Great riches, unfortunately, tend to bring out the worst in most individuals. Pure lust and greed preclude any normal instincts to share and prove how utterly egocentric individuals can be. Wealth is meant to be shared, as is knowledge – which may be the true underlying significance of a dragon's treasure. Hoarding either one may make a person feel powerful but when one is so selfish as to keep gifts hidden from others, he only serves to alienate himself. What good are riches or knowledge if you have no one with whom to share them?

The dragons in this scene may appear to have thick skin, but rest assured that they also have weak spots that are vulnerable to pain. No matter how resistant one believes he is to injury, no one is immune to suffering or the misery brought on by loneliness.

The Three of Swords indicates a separation due to strife. Hatred, quarreling, and base instincts are represented by this card. Upheavals may be expected and physical or emotional injury may occur.

Reversed Meaning: *Illness. Confusion. Chaos. Estrangement. Hostility. War.*

A reversal of the Three of Swords carries much the same meaning as its upright position, but to an even greater degree. Greed and jealousy may cause insanity; confusion and mistakes result in chaos; hatred and alienation lead to loneliness and misery. Lording one's possessions over others impresses no one and causes resentment, possibly leading to all-out war.

The appearance of this card in a reading may indicate a need to evaluate how much one values material possessions over people. Remember the old adage: *You can't take it with you.*

FOUR OF SWORDS

4 Swords

Meaning: *Solitude. Refuge. Exile. Respite.*

Will-o'-the-wisp are believed to haunt lonely places and myriad hypotheses exist as to what may be the source of these mysterious Faery lights which hover so near the ground. Some people view will-o'-the-wisp as a portent of good fortune, believing the diminutive glowing orbs gather near buried treasure. Others consider them bad omens, foreshadowing death or perhaps even *causing* death by luring unsuspecting travelers away from the safety of well-trodden paths into unknown and dangerous regions. Their eerie presence envelops one with a sense of lethargy and isolation, blocking out the desire to reason or act of one's own accord.

In this card, the enigmatic Faery lights hover near a sword thrust into the ground by a leafless tree. Perhaps the tree is dead, along with the owner of the sword. Or perhaps the tree is simply taking its winter's rest as the owner of the sword wanders dazedly, alone and unarmed, through the night. Whatever the case, a sense of solitude and foreboding accompany this card.

The Four of Swords indicates rest after a period of strife. The seclusion evident in this card expresses a sense of exile or banishment. Respite is available now but it carries with it a feeling of loneliness. Do not allow your imagination to wander like the illusory will-o'-the-wisp. Even though you may feel isolated, there is an entire world outside, just waiting for your return. Although the ebony blackness appears endless, the will-o'-the-wisp offers sparks of light to brighten the darkness, providing hope for the new day that will dawn.

Reversed Meaning: *Slow recovery. Inability to rest easy. Exercise caution.*

The Four of Swords reversed may indicate a slow but steady recovery from illness, loss, or a bad experience. There is light at the end of the tunnel, but caution must still be used in order to regain one's former strength and standing. This includes listening to doctor's advice and taking care of one's physical and mental health.

A reversal of the Four of Swords may signify an inability to rest at ease due to insomnia or unpleasant dreams. This card relates to dreaming and the astral plane, so conscious problems may be trying to solve themselves through subconscious means. Pay attention to dreams and allow your intuitive mind the freedom required to repair the problem.

FIVE OF SWORDS

5 Swords

Meaning: *Arguments. Defeat. Misery. Unfair attack. Gain through the misfortune of others. No-win situation. Destruction. Shame.*

Jenny Greenteeth was once a favorite threat used by mothers to keep their children from wandering too near the banks of water sources lest they be dragged down into her watery, slime-ridden domain. Jenny was but one of countless deadly water fairies whose primary pleasure lay in taking away the lives of others, regardless of their status or innocence.

In this card, Jenny adds another ill-gotten sword to her collection, thrusting it into the muddy banks of her lair as a trophy of her latest conquest. Herein lies a warning for her hapless victims. Not only were the owners of these swords aware of Jenny's treacherous actions through the lore of their childhood; they failed to heed the obvious signs that others had already fallen prey to the clutches of this lethal fairy being. Some people never seem to learn and feel themselves invincible even in the face of certain danger.

Jenny, however, cares naught for the heroics of men or even the innocence of children. Her ways are deceitful and unfair. Those who venture too close to Jenny's grasp are walking into a no-win situation. Shame, degradation, and most likely death are all the future will hold for them.

It is unwise to deliberately cross such a dangerous and untrustworthy individual who gains from the misfortune of others. Such personalities should be avoided, rather than foolishly taunted into deadly action.

This is a card of misfortune and shame that may only be avoided if a concerted effort is made to steer clear of such obvious danger. Still, some perils lie hidden, surprising us when we least expect it. This card is a warning of imminent risk and it represents a situation that will most likely prove overwhelming and disastrous, if not fatal.

Reversed Meaning: *Mourning. Pain. Sorrow. Distress. Vengeance.*

The Five of Swords reversed bodes even worse than the upright card which serves as a warning to avoid a desperate situation. This position represents mourning for one already lost and is indicative of funerals and burial. It is a card full of pain and distress, sorrows, and remorse. One may have hope for vengeance, but this will accomplish nothing, save causing one to sink further into the depths of confusion and despair. It is a dark card, but one must bear in mind that once things have hit rock bottom, they can only get better.

SIX OF SWORDS

6 Swords

Meaning: *Light in Darkness. Passage out of troubles and sorrow. Journey may bring peace and harmony.*

The Snow Queen glides across the frigid waters of her Arctic home toward the luminous beauty of the aurora borealis. Behind her, swords stand frozen in the snow and ice, illustrative of the unyielding rigidity of an aggressive past. As water is symbolic of spiritual matters, the frozen land of ice behind her is indicative of a spiritually frozen attitude, one that has no movement or warmth and therefore can develop no further.

Because of this realization, the Snow Queen has taken her boat upon the waters that will allow her to drift into other lands, discovering new environments that may help her deepen her sensibilities and spirituality. She heads toward the glow of the mysterious aurora borealis, leaving the darkness and cold of the past behind her. Note, however, that she still grasps a sword for protection, not knowing what, if any, dangers she may encounter on her journey.

The Six of Swords indicates a journey by water, as well as a passage from trouble and sorrow into a brighter, more hopeful, future. Spiritual sojourns and travels on the astral plane may take on a more important role, as a move is made from the turmoil of the past into a more peaceful state of being. Better circumstances lie ahead. However, one would be wise to remain on guard and keep defenses in place should necessity call for them.

Reversed Meaning: *Journey postponed. No immediate way out of present difficulties.*

A reversal of the Six of Swords indicates that one may be unable to leave a difficult situation, either from obstacles blocking one's path, or from fear of what the future may hold. Delays and changes of plans are likely and it may feel as though you are fighting against the current.

Like the Snow Queen, you may be cold and aloof, indifferent to possibilities of change that lie before you. It is comforting to continue a pattern of thought or behavior that seems to have sustained you thus far in your life. But now is a time for change – to move past ideas and behaviors that no longer benefit the development of your soul. It is time to let the warm undercurrents of spirituality flow through you and melt the icy defenses you have built inside yourself. Leave the darkness of your past behind you and let your soul drift to the radiant luminosity of the One Being. That is where you will find serenity, peace, and love.

SEVEN OF SWORDS ══════════

7 Swords

Meaning: *Perseverance. Light of Hope. The worst is behind you. Flight from dishonorable actions. Theft. Betrayal. Journey by land.*

Caves are a favorite haunt for creatures of Faery, but the nymph pictured has sought the enveloping darkness of a cave out of fear and shame, rather than for shelter. Perhaps she has stolen something from mortals – a favorite pastime – betrayed a friend, or committed some other dishonest act she now regrets and seeks to avoid. This card represents flight from actions one would rather not face but it also indicates the use of one's mind to reason out the situation and overcome anxieties and fears.

Grasping her knees to herself in a gesture of security and protection, this fairy indicates that she actually feels neither. Her timid smile hints at her remorse for whatever has caused her retreat into the safety and anonymity provided by the depths of the cave. Swords line the steps behind her, signaling that her troubles are now in the past. A small square of light touches the stones next to her, while an even greater glow envelops the fairy herself, proving that there is light at the end of the tunnel.

The Seven of Swords carries with it not only the awareness of transgressions but also the ability to admit responsibility for them, atone for them, and move on. It could also indicate a journey by land or traveling incognito.

Reversed Meaning: *Temporary setbacks. Discretion. Dishonesty revealed.*

A reversal of this card indicates the desire to avoid trouble and to live life openly and honestly, rather than in fear. More care is taken now, perhaps from concern over getting caught, but this prudence will be well worth the effort.

Good advice is given – *heed it!* Setbacks may impede your path, but they will only be temporary. If you have nothing to hide, then you have nothing to fear. Things are actually turning around for you.

EIGHT OF SWORDS

Meaning: *Self-imposed restrictions. Trials. Condemnation. Imprisonment. The need to be rescued. Feelings of depression and anxiety.*

A dwarf works hard at tempering yet another finely wrought blade. Evidence of his skill and patience abounds in his workshop full of swords. Still, the grouping of weapons around him suggests a prison. Perhaps the dwarf feels overburdened by his task or maybe he wishes to do something totally different with his talents.

The Eight of Swords indicates self-imposed constraints and a feeling of being held captive by them. Quite often, when we are good at doing something, we are called upon to perform it regularly by others. It is nice to have one's talents acknowledged; however, it is rather unpleasant to feel taken advantage of by having to utilize those abilities so often, especially when there are other things we would rather be doing. Not allowing ourselves the time to do things we *really* wish to do can lead to feelings of anxiety and depression. We all need to step out of our shell at times and this card suggests you give yourself permission to do that.

This is not an inescapable position. This card implies that the querent has put himself into a situation from which only *he* can release himself. Maybe a need to be rescued by someone else is felt, but it is time to realize that is not possible since the circumstances are self-created. In fact, if other cards suggest the querent is actually imprisoned or has done something wrong, he needs to take responsibility for his actions and atone for them. We are the only ones who can truly condemn ourselves and seeking to make amends will relieve us of our burdens.

Reversed Meaning: *Misfortune. Self-sabotage. Gullible nature could lead to being easily deceived. Resourcefulness may help correct a bad situation.*

The Eight of Swords in a reversed position indicates that one may encounter great difficulties and that much work may be needed to resolve problems. It is time to use one's ingenuity to remedy the situation.

Since the Eight of Swords suggests a self-created cage or prison of some sort, its reversal may be a warning that one has naively put up barriers to understanding, causing gullibility and confusion. We cannot remain protected behind a safety screen forever, and now may be the time to take down those walls.

NINE OF SWORDS

9 Swords

Meaning: *Danger. Despair. Doubt. Isolation.*

A lone traveler guardedly raises his sword as he passes through a dark forest surrounded by Ghillie Dhu. These are rather dangerous elves that live in birch trees and derive pleasure from accosting and possibly enslaving hapless victims who wander through their domain. While the traveler cannot actually see the Ghillie Dhu, he obviously senses a threatening presence and has wisely drawn his sword for protection.

Because of his solitude, the man may mistrust his own instincts and abilities, putting himself at greater risk of danger from the Ghillie Dhu. Obviously, his mind is not simply playing a trick on him. The peril is very real, even though he cannot physically see it. The man needs to set aside his doubt and proceed through the wood with confidence so the Ghillie Dhu will not be able to take advantage of his insecurities.

When this card appears in a reading, it implies a sense of loneliness, isolation, self-pity, and suspicion. Fears may be all in one's mind, but this is not the time to doubt. Whether or not danger is real, fears need to be faced head on and overcome. One's own sense of self-worth needs to be brought to the fore so that feelings of failure, loss, and anxiety do not lead to depression. Be on guard and remain ready to take action.

Reversed Meaning: *The nightmare is over. Difficulty seeing a project through to the end. Spiritual struggle.*

A reversal of the Nine of Swords indicates that one is coming out of a depression and things are improving. The memory of past disappointments and feelings of impotence may linger, making it difficult to muster the energy and resolve to see projects through to the end without giving up at this time.

Fears and suspicions experienced now may be perfectly legitimate so one should remain vigilant. Any feelings of shame or disgrace should be disregarded. Try to hold your head high and look beyond the present situation. The nightmare is now over and better dreams will come.

TEN OF SWORDS

10 Swords

Meaning: *Enemies. Failure. Desolation. Suffering.*

The Unseelie Court are air spirits who traverse the night winds searching for hapless mortals to enslave. In this scene, one of their dreaded assembly hovers over a desolate battlefield, mockingly carrying a battle standard whose pennant has taken on the shape of an ominous red lightning bolt. The field is littered with the corpses of soldiers – a pleasant sight for this macabre phantom. If he cannot bind mortals to his twisted will, then his next best option is to see them dead.

This is a card of unforeseen disaster and suffering. The deceased men in this picture may have been allies or sworn enemies. However, their allegiance in life is now a moot point as they have all become the same in death. Their glorious attempts at victory led them to nothing but an early grave. For the Unseelie Court and other dark spirits, this is a joyous occasion since it has hastened their work of spreading desolation throughout the world.

The appearance of this card in a reading heralds tragedy and misery. Enemies are simply waiting for your downfall and your own fear of failure will only add to the disaster.

The Ten of Swords indicates a need for power, even if many individuals must suffer so that one may feel superior. Whatever control is gained will be fleeting. The desire to battle others for personal reasons will avail you nothing.

Reversed Meaning: *Power. Temporary advantage. Momentary triumph.*

Although the Ten of Swords is a card of sadness and woe in its upright position, a reversal of this card brings a glimmer of hope. One may be able to gain a temporary advantage in a situation due to the kindness or grace of another individual. Still, this may be only a passing success or a slight recovery. Circumstances may be terrible for a while but hold your head high and remember that nothing lasts forever.

PAGE OF SWORDS

Page of Swords

Meaning: *Curiosity. Knowledge. Secrecy. Observation. Vigilance.*

The Page of Swords is a beautiful youth with the world at his fingertips. A brilliant observer with an inquisitive mind, the Page seeks information wherever he can find it. One should remain alert in his presence however, for the Page is not above using personal knowledge of others to his advantage when it suits him.

The Page is clever and shrewd, taking in everything around him and capable of rapid response in any given situation. Because of his love of learning, he may be quite talented and conversant in many areas. Others see him as a precocious child, albeit one to remain vigilant around. He can be quite spiteful and petulant if he perceives that he has been threatened or wronged in any way.

The Page of Swords in a reading refers to a person with such character traits and may indicate a scholar, scientist, or actor. It may signify a need to become more attuned to your surroundings so that no surprises catch you off guard. This includes watching what you say and do lest another observant person discover something that may be used against you.

The Page of Swords is a card of spying, secrecy, and knowledge. The ability to blend in well has its advantages as one may be able obtain information from close proximity to others. Ulterior motives are likely and discretion should be used. Knowledge can be a two-edged sword, especially when employed for personal ends. Be aware that others are watching you, and that your conduct may determine whether you gain their respect or are marked by them for easy manipulation.

Reversed Meaning: *Impostor. Weakness. Plots. Being caught unawares. Difficulty fitting in.*

A reversal of the Page of Swords may indicate a weak person, both in terms of character and physical make-up. Someone may not be who he seems. Instead, he may be an impostor acting out a role to perfection in order to ensnare others. A plot or attack may be underway with the perpetrator simply awaiting the appropriate moment to strike.

The Page of Swords reversed also may suggest a person who bears severe wounds from childhood which made him the person he is today. Past physical or mental abuse may have traumatized this person, making him wary and defensive, perhaps denying him the ability to speak for himself or deal well with others.

PRINCE OF SWORDS

Prince of Swords

Meaning: *Military prowess. Courage. Enemy. Bully. Opposition. Anger. Destruction.*

The Prince of Swords stands calmly with sword raised. Impassive, he presents the image of a cool, dominant personality. The Prince is a powerful warrior – brave, strong, and highly intelligent. He has no fear and would gladly serve as a soldier, easily taking on the role of commander. His passion for adventure and danger prompt him to seek exploits that would cause trepidation in others. Most people would consider him to be a dashing and heroic figure because of his courageousness, yet he has none of the gallantry or selflessness of a true hero. In fact, whatever he does is more for his own sense of self-worth and honor than for humanitarian reasons.

Although the Prince is the epitome of skill and bravery, he can also be extremely vindictive and cruel. Beware his wrath. Once angered, he becomes an implacable foe. Always resting beneath the surface of the Prince's handsome exterior are feelings of hatred and enmity, simply waiting for a chance to be released.

This card represents a spoiled, conceited individual who is used to having his own way and is prepared to get it by ruthless means if necessary. Even those who call themselves his friends are not immune to his dangerous nature and vengeful actions. He is a person who "shoots first and asks questions later." No matter whether one is friend or foe, the Prince has no patience and will do whatever he feels best serves his purposes at the moment.

Rather than face his own faults, he prefers to shift the blame to others. The Prince refuses to see the error of his ways and he has convinced himself that the world is simply unjust to him. Hence, he uses his power to take revenge for real or imagined slights. He will not listen to reason, especially in his fury.

The appearance of the Prince of Swords in a reading suggests a person with his qualities may be entering the picture. If so, prudence dictates that one take care not to offend a person of such disposition – this could be a dreadful mistake.

Opposition may be blocking one's path. At this time, it may be best to turn the other way to avoid a deadly confrontation. We should always have the fortitude to stand our ground, but sometimes it is unwise to push a given situation.

Reversed Meaning: *Conceit. Ignorance. Foolishness. Impulsiveness. Fury.*

A reversal of the Prince of Swords implies foolhardiness. One may rush headlong into a dangerous situation with no thought given to facts or the possible outcome of such a rash decision.

This card may indicate disaster. If a calamity occurs, it is best to react in a calm, reasonable manner. Getting irritated and using a bad situation as a chance to vent your frustration only makes matters worse.

QUEEN OF SWORDS

Meaning: *Detached. Candid. Separation. Sorrow. Widow.*

The Queen of Swords is a proud woman, strong in her beliefs and prepared to fight for the truth as she perceives it. She is unflinching in the face of loss and disaster, having personally experienced immense pain from both in the past.

The Queen of Swords may represent a widow, divorcee, or spinster. She is alone at present and perhaps somewhat bitter over her circumstances. Yet she is strong enough to remain resolute and move forward with her life. In truth, being on her own allows the Queen the opportunity to really be herself, rather than adjusting her life to merge with that of another.

The Queen is a highly intelligent and complex being. Her lofty ideals and depth of mind may cause her to seem aloof and uncaring to those who cannot fathom her complex nature. She is a very direct person and not given to kind and soothing words, although she truly means to be helpful in her criticisms of others. She says and does only what she feels is right and of benefit to all.

The Queen's familiar is a salamander which is a fire elemental that reflects her personality. Like the salamander, the Queen is extremely capable of adapting to situations and has no fear of the flames of adversity. In fact, pain and devastation only make her grow stronger. The Queen has known great sorrow but she has learned to distance herself from her emotions in order to better perceive circumstances and handle them in the most effective manner.

The appearance of the Queen in a reading signifies someone with her personality attributes. It may mean that a situation needs to be handled with a calm, reserved, and detached approach. Perhaps it infers that you need to look deeper than surface level at someone considered to be cold and harsh. That person may actually be quite deep and caring. Sometimes we are very hard on those we love and expect more of them because we want more for them.

Reversed Meaning: *Wicked. Spiteful. Hypocrite. Fanaticism. Narrow-minded. Solitude.*

The Queen of Swords reversed may indicate a frustrated and vengeful person who seeks not only to make her own life better, but also to gain revenge on those she feels have wronged her. She may easily become fanatical in her beliefs. Or worse yet, she may be hypocritical and refuse to judge herself by the rigid views and behaviors she expects of others.

The Queen may represent a wicked and spiteful person who will use deception to make a situation turn her way. This is a woman not afraid to cry rape or fake a pregnancy if she thinks it will help her gain what she desires.

KING OF SWORDS

King of Swords

Meaning: *Leadership. Power. Intelligence. Logic. Fairness.*

The King of Swords is a powerful figure who readily commands respect for his authority. He is a born leader and may represent a high ranking political figure, military commander, judge, man of the cloth, or business leader. The king is just, reasonable, and extremely logical, although somewhat dispassionate. Because of this, he has a tendency to be rather skeptical, preferring to ignore the human and emotional substance of a matter in favor of solid facts.

The King of Swords is inclined to be suspicious and overly cautious and he never proceeds impulsively into a situation. He is a man of high ideals and even temperament, although he can be quite formidable if roused to anger. Still, he prefers a peaceful existence and will only revert to the sword in the direst of circumstances.

The King of Swords is accustomed to getting his way and he uses logic to justify his requirements. As a parent, he is strict and critical but only because he wants his children to be as honest, fair, and intelligent as himself. He expects nothing of others he is not prepared to do himself and he would willingly sacrifice his own life for the sake of his subjects.

The appearance of the King of Swords in a reading suggests a person of his character. It may signify a time to be strict but fair. Good leadership is necessary.

Reversed Meaning: *Strict disciplinarian. Enemy. Evil intentions. Sadistic behavior.*

The King of Swords reversed may indicate conflict and that someone has an unfair advantage. This card represents a cold-hearted disciplinarian who is unsympathetic and inhumane. He not only *wants* his own way but he *gets* it by any means necessary including excessive cruelty.

A reversal of this card may refer to an influential person whose logic has degenerated, causing him to view wickedness and perversions as nothing out of the ordinary. He cares only for his own personal desires and will stop at nothing to attain them.

Wands

ACE OF WANDS

Ace of Wands

Meaning: *Beginnings. Birth. Time for action. Go for your goal.*

The Ace of Wands is a card of beginnings. It may possibly refer to an actual birth, but most likely, it heralds the birth of an idea or action. It is time for a fresh start and to set new goals – time to go for it!

This card is full of energy. Like a real wand, it urges you to focus your intentions and energy toward your desire and *will* it into existence. *Your own will* is the key to this card. The Ace is full of possibilities, welcoming you into new adventures and opportunities. The perfect time to seize your dream is *now*. Everything is in order, lined up and waiting for your personal desire to help manifest it.

When the Ace of Wands appears in a reading, it is a time to reach for the stars and take advantage of all life is offering you. If there is something you have wanted to do but have hesitated for various reasons, then give it a try now. There is nothing to be lost.

The Ace of Wands is a happy card, full of promise for the future. Focusing your intentions and directing them to a desired outcome will produce positive results.

Reversed Meaning: *Laziness. Impotence. Bad start. Lack of desire.*

A reversal of the Ace of Wands indicates a lack of will to see things through to the end. Focus is gone, energies are scattered, and there is simply no desire to continue putting effort into a planned undertaking.

Perhaps one simply got off to a poor start or felt that it was too soon or too late to try something new. Since the Wands represent *will*, a desire to accomplish things is necessary in order to succeed. In a reversed position, the will is lacking and plans are best left on hold until the conscious intent is regained. One should take this time for introspection to try to understand why the desire is not there. Understanding brings peace, peace offers hope, and hope inspires will.

TWO OF WANDS

2 Wands

Meaning: *Creative ability. Growth. Melancholy.*

In this scene, a fairy uses her wands to aid in the growth of a hosta plant. She balances on a leaf, focusing her energies through the wands and into the plant. This is not only her duty but also her way of giving back to the universe. She is creating beauty and caring for it within her little corner of the world.

The Two of Wands signifies the use of one's creative abilities to aid enterprise. This could relate to a current job, project, or even the raising of a family.

Vast amounts of energy are implied by this card but an element of melancholy also accompanies it. The fairy knows that even with all her efforts, the hosta must ultimately wither and die only to be reborn and nurtured by her again the next year. In the same way, parents raise their children in the knowledge that they must one day venture out on their own, hopefully returning in time with their own children. Even business moguls know they must one day retire and hand the reins of their enterprise over to a capable successor.

Occasionally, it seems that all the time and energy we invest in undertakings is for nothing. But we need to remain aware of the fact that all the love and effort we pour into any task is of enormous import. We should be proud of all we have accomplished. Creating a thing of beauty and promise is a wonderful achievement, something to take pride in – even when it is time to let go.

Reversed Meaning: *Rapture. Enchantment. New Beginnings that may not be productive.*

A reversal of the Two of Wands implies a sense of awe and wonder – pure joy for all that exists. A true understanding of the import of one's place in the Universe is enlightening and inspiring.

This is a time for new beginnings, although plans may not immediately bear fruit. Be patient, while continuing to revel in the in the splendor and awesome magnificence of creation.

THREE OF WANDS

3 Wands

Meaning: *Cooperation. Partnership. Initiative. Foresight.*

The Three of Wands represents cooperation. Quite often, we feel it is easier to do things on our own; however, if we work in concert with others, matters tend to get taken care of much more quickly and efficiently.

Partnering with others, or at least the willingness to accept help or advice from someone else, will not only move a project along but it will give one the chance to become closer to another individual. While it is nice to take pride in a task accomplished completely on one's own, it is just as satisfying to share the honor for a job well done.

The appearance of the Three of Wands in a reading indicates that cooperation is necessary, especially in business matters. Initiative is called for and travel may be involved in the project. Foresight will aid in the accomplishment of tasks.

Reversed Meaning: *Respite. Daydreaming. Ignoring issues. Creative block.*

The fairy pictured in this card gives the impression of calm and balance. In reality, she has turned her back on a situation, ignoring what she does not wish to face. She sits alone, lost in her own world of daydreams, waiting for things to happen on their own.

The Three of Wands reversed may indicate a creative block or the unwillingness to deal with others. Stepping back from the situation may help one get thoughts in order, but this respite must eventually end so that work may be accomplished. Working in collaboration with others is the quickest way to complete a job. You may be surprised how listening to the ideas of others causes your own to blossom.

FOUR OF WANDS

4 Wands

Meaning: *Achievement. Peace. Happiness. Beauty of home.*

This card pictures two fairies congratulating one another on a job well done, helping Indian Pipe plants to grow. The Indian Pipe, or Corpse Plant, lives in intimate association with subterranean fungi that take nourishment from the roots of decaying trees. Like the Indian Pipe, these fairies take sustenance from everything within their universe and try to give back what they can.

Human beings are no different in the intricate relationships of their lives. We all need to help one another to sustain life on this planet. Even those we do not outwardly recognize as being of immediate assistance to us are still there behind the scenes, helping make our lives run more smoothly.

The Four of Wands in a reading suggests achievement and the peace and happiness experienced from a job well done. This is a time for individuals to reward themselves for their labors and to recognize and thank others for *their* assistance.

The Four of Wands may indicate a marriage or a homecoming. We must remember to give thanks for all the bounty given to us each day.

Reversed Meaning: *Lack of pleasure. Feeling that something is missing.*

A reversal of the Four of Wands does not really carry a negative connotation, but it does include the aspect of incompleteness. One may have the world at his fingertips, yet there is a lingering feeling that something is missing.

This emotion is quite often experienced at the holidays, when entire families gather to celebrate the season and their love for one another. Sometimes, when we view the joy of others and hear of their accomplishments, we tend to forget about our own blessings and we feel less important. This card reminds us to be grateful for everything *we* have – family, friends, health, home, job. Even the smallest things in life are great gifts that should be acknowledged and not taken for granted.

FIVE OF WANDS

5 Wands

Meaning: *Obstacles. Conflict. Power struggle. Law suits.*

The Five of Wands depicts Rubezahl guarding their mountain pass with slender, spiked walking staffs. The Rubezahl are male dwarf fairies of Eastern European origin who haunt seldom-used roads in order to cause trouble for travelers. Sometimes they have been known to help the lost – especially children. But they derive far more pleasure from playing tricks on those who venture across their paths.

The Five of Wands in a reading indicates that obstacles are blocking one's path. Strife is present, and you may have to fight for what you perceive to be right. A lawsuit may be possible at this time. You must be courageous and do your utmost to prove yourself to others, lest they take advantage of you.

This card carries with it the love of games and exercise, but it warns that playful actions can quickly escalate into hostilities. Competition is strong, and you must behave in a sportsmanlike manner. Power struggles are evident. Pride and ambition exist on both sides of an argument, and you must remain aware of that fact and be sensitive to the feelings of others. You must also be cognizant of the fact that too much pride and ambition are tantamount to arrogance, which can easily destroy any good thing you have going for yourself.

Reversed Meaning: *Disputes. Disagreements. Delays.*

The Five of Wands in a reversed position suggests that your anxieties are coming to an end but you may still need some help from others. There may continue to be delays and discomfort but the situation will gradually improve.

Although the Five of Wands indicates a love of exercise and games, a reversal of this card implies that one is tired of playing games – either literally or figuratively – and wants to be left alone. This card could indicate harassment and quarrels. You need to stand your ground and remain firm in your beliefs in order to prevail.

SIX OF WANDS

6 Wands

Meaning: *Victory. Good news. Helpful friends. Possible journey.*

The Six of Wands depicts the mythical Firebird holding six feathers she is prepared to give as a means of calling on her when help is needed. The Firebird is a proud and noble creature, albeit one that is not overly fond of human beings. Still, the Firebird, if captured, is willing to lend her strength and magical powers to the one fortunate enough to gain control over her. She may not do so cheerfully, but she has great honor and will not back out of her promise.

The Six of Wands indicates victory. Great success will be achieved, especially with the assistance of reliable friends. Harmonious relationships bring out the best in people, allowing them to work together for the common good. Much will be accomplished through teamwork.

A journey is likely, particularly one involving a leadership role. This may take the form of something such as an actual business trip or it could more figuratively refer to a spiritual journey of self-empowerment. Whatever the case, this is a time for hope and advancement.

Reversed Meaning: *Insolence. Arrogance. Poor loser. Journey postponed.*

A reversal of the Six of Wands suggests that victory will be fleeting, or simply may not occur at all. Arrogance is your worst enemy, causing you to become overly confident in your abilities. Not only may others be disrespectful of your authority; they could perhaps even become treacherous to the point of betrayal.

The Six of Wands reversed implies a fall from high places, brought about by one's own pride. Jealously of those in a winning position is likely and reactions to their triumph may take on a less than sporting attitude.

Journeys may be postponed or other delays may prevent one from accomplishing a given task. Leadership skills have reached a rather low ebb at the moment, and one should take account of how he deals with those in a subordinate position.

SEVEN OF WANDS

Meaning: *Prevailing against all odds. High productivity. Success. Profit.*

Reversed Meaning: *Being taken advantage of. Feeling overwhelmed. Embarrassment.*

The Seven of Wands portrays Rumpelstiltskin approaching the miller's daughter just as she was about to give up hope of ever being able to accede to her father's boast that she could spin straw into gold. Those familiar with the fairy tale know that if the girl failed to produce gold for the king, she or her father would face execution. Facing such an ignominious fate, the miller's daughter had little option but to bargain with the gnome, Rumpelstiltskin, who accomplished the task for her.

The Seven of Wands in a reading indicates success against all odds. Competition is stiff, and many obstacles block one's path. However, with fortitude and perseverance, victory will be achieved, high levels of productivity will be realized, and a great deal of profit will ensue.

Rumpelstiltskin held up his end of the deal with the miller's daughter by spinning three rooms full of gold for the girl who was then married to the king. After the birth of her first child, Rumpelstiltskin returned to collect the baby as payment for his services, just as the miller's daughter had originally agreed. Needless to say, she had a change of heart and refused to give up her child to the gnome. Rumpelstiltskin gave her a chance to keep the baby if she could guess his name. The queen, of course, managed to learn his name, and in a fit of pique, Rumpelstiltskin stomped through the floor and was never seen again.

A reversal of the Seven of Wands warns against letting others take advantage of you. You may feel overwhelmed, yet responsible for a situation into which you have been thrust. Someone may try to coax you into doing something through pleading or threats but you need to hold your ground.

Embarrassment may occur causing you to lash out at others to compensate for feelings of vulnerability. Composure and patience are needed at this time in order to see a project through bit by bit. Do not let others force you into rushing, or into any situation that you really do not feel equipped to handle at the moment.

105

EIGHT OF WANDS

8 Wands

Meaning: *Nearing a goal. Arrows of love find mark. Journey by air.*

The Eight of Wands depicts Cupid preparing to shoot an arrow at an idyllic couple relaxing in a garden. This card represents romance and the beautiful things in life, especially nature.

This is a time to be swept off one's feet, either by love or by the pure joy of existence. The Eight of Wands signifies a love of the outdoors, especially in open places where people can gather for fun and frolic. It may also connote a journey by air.

The Eight of Wands indicates that the arrows of love have found their mark. It also carries the idea that one has aimed for a chosen goal and it is about to be met. Energies are increasing and becoming more focused now, although an element of haste is implied. One must take care not to move too quickly or force a situation.

Reversed Meaning: *Jealousy. Domestic disputes. Communications go astray.*

The Eight of Wands in a reversed position suggests that a situation has been forced and is on the verge of falling apart. This could refer to any number of circumstances but especially those related to romance. Perhaps the person of one's dreams does not reciprocate those feelings or maybe jealousy has reared its ugly head and brought about domestic disputes and even violence.

Incompatibility is a feature of the Eight of Wand's reversal. This could stem from two conflicting natures or it may simply be from a miscommunication of thoughts and ideals.

The energy implied by the upright position of this card is, in effect, wasted in the reversal. Too much haste has spent the dynamic spirit of one's efforts, and from this point, vitality will only wane. Delays and cancellations may occur as things start to slow down.

NINE OF WANDS

9 Wands

Meaning: *Defensiveness. Preparedness. Stubbornness. Health. Strength in reserve.*

A deer-like fairy gazes warily over her shoulder. The tips of her antlers glow slightly, a signal that she is preparing to either attack or run away. In her own element, she is strong and in control. Those who trespass or threaten her in any way are likely to bear the brunt of her antlers.

The Nine of Wands indicates a defensive stance that may serve one well. It is always best to be prepared and remain on one's guard, especially when dealing with the unknown. Still, this card represents a tendency toward stubbornness, which may be unnecessary in the given situation.

This card in its upright position represents health and a strong-willed individual of good moral character. It suggests suspicion of others, either from instinctual feelings or from past experience. One may need to wait a bit to see how things will turn out, but be prepared for any eventuality.

Reversed Meaning: *Unpreparedness. Weak character. Poor health.*

A reversal of the Nine of Wands indicates that one may not be ready for events that may ensue. It could imply ill health, or merely a desire to avoid responsibilities.

Obstacles are probably hindering progress and it may be time to attack the problem head on. One might be overly defensive about an issue or perhaps caught off guard. Delays are likely, especially as doubts and mistrust exist.

TEN OF WANDS

10 Wands

Meaning: *Burden. Burnout. Betrayal.*

A fairy gazes dejectedly at her wand, aware that her energy has waned and her powers have been depleted. Even her drooping wings have lost their color and the tree she was meant to care for has become thorny and bare as it, too, succumbs to the lifelessness the fairy currently feels.

This card represents overwhelming responsibilities and the lack of power one feels in handling them. It signifies tiredness, burnout, and a strong desire to simply leave a situation entirely.

Complete disruption of life and failure to see things through have brought on a sense of betrayal by those who have relied on one for support. Great resentment may be felt toward those that one serves. A sense of being trapped or pushed beyond the limits one can bear has taken over and all delight has faded away.

Reversed Meaning: *Efforts directed toward selfish ends. Loss. Worry.*

A reversal of the Ten of Wands indicates denial about how difficult a situation is, even though results are proving that tasks are outside the realm of one's control or abilities. This card may represent a person who tends to shift blame or burden onto others or who directs his own efforts toward selfish ends.

Nothing is being accomplished at present because the desire is simply lacking. One may worry over the outcome of a situation, but events are not controllable and the outcome is not favorable. Be prepared to face a loss because the will to sustain a situation is gone.

PAGE OF WANDS

Page of Wands.

Meaning: *Brilliance. Candor. Fearlessness. Zealous personality.*

The Page of Wands is a vibrant, passionate individual with an impetuous nature and a mind ever in search of knowledge. Because of the pure zeal embodied in the Page, the quest for information on any subject can easily turn obsessive. This is the personality of an ardent fan who just cannot seem to get enough.

The Page of Wands dives headlong into a chosen project, researching every aspect of it until there is nothing more to learn. Because of this, the Page has a wealth of knowledge about many subjects and makes an excellent conversationalist. The Page loves to explore things in depth, and ideas or subjects that others may find too mundane or unusual intrigue the Page.

Since the Page of Wands is fearless and possessed by a need to know the inner workings of practically everything – including self – she is willing to try just about anything. The Page is a very candid individual due to the courage and capriciousness of character embodied in this personality.

The appearance of the Page of Wands in a reading relates to a person with her characteristics. It may also indicate the arrival of unexpected messages, heralding the need for prompt action. This news will not necessarily be bad. In fact, it will more than likely instigate positive change in one's life.

Reversed Meaning: *Temperamental. Melodramatic. Indecision. Bad news.*

The Page of Wands reversed indicates a temperamental individual who is apt to throw a tantrum if she does not get her way. The Page may be bored or simply not in the mood to do something, with no consideration for the feelings or wishes of others regarding the matter.

In a reversed position, the Page of Wands might tend to make rash decisions that show a lack of judgment. Because she so fervently examines every aspect of a given topic, the Page may experience burnout from obsessive searching and become bored with details and monotony. Since this person may suffer from hyperactivity and/or an attention deficit disorder, she needs to be careful not to take on more than she can handle.

PRINCE OF WANDS

Prince of Wands

Meaning: *Impetuous nature. Adventurer. Rebel. Capriciousness.*

The Prince of Wands is represented by Robin Goodfellow, a mischievous nature sprite also known as Puck. Like Robin/Puck, the Prince of Wands is basically a very nice sort of fellow, although given to knavish behavior at the slightest whim.

The Prince of Wands has a highly impetuous nature which leads him to continually explore new places and ideas. He is a grand adventurer, seeking out pleasure and dare-deviltry whenever and wherever possible. Bold, passionate, and daring, the Prince does not hesitate to jump headlong into any situation.

As a friend or lover, the Prince is more than generous. His friends, however, need to beware his competitive nature. The Prince enjoys a friendly rivalry which may go a bit too far. His lovers need be even more wary. While he can be an ardent lover, the last thing the Prince of Wands desires is commitment.

The Prince's lack of dedication spills over into almost every aspect of his life. Although he may be totally enthusiastic at the start of any undertaking, his interest quickly wanes and boredom forces him to forego finishing any project.

The Prince of Wands definitely has a rebellious nature where staid behavior and conformity to rules are concerned. He always looks to the future and has no appreciation for what he considers outmoded. These characteristics, however, cause him to be an innovative thinker with new solutions to old problems.

The Prince of Wands in a reading suggests a person of his character and temperament. The appearance of this card may indicate an impending journey that will expose the querent to new ideas and experiences.

Reversed Meaning: *Conflict. Impatience. Lack of Focus. Journey delayed.*

The Prince of Wands in a reversed position increases the negative aspects of a regular reading. A playful rivalry may turn into out and out conflict or a lack of devotion toward a lover may turn to jealousy. A rebellious nature may be without focus or an outlet, thus causing the perpetration of mischievous or even malevolent acts.

In a reversal, the Prince of Wands becomes far more of a rogue and trickster than in the upright position. His impatience causes extremely hasty actions which result in adversity for those around him. Journeys will be delayed.

QUEEN OF WANDS

Queen of Wands

Meaning: *Romantic. Optimistic. Love of Nature. Influential Leader.*

The Queen of Wands is a powerfully attractive, vivacious personality. She is pictured with her crow familiar. The crow is a symbol of the spiritual realm especially as it relates to death. The crow is linked with the element of *ether,* or spirit, even more than it is associated with air, the element represented by the suit of Wands. This connection to the spirit realm enhances the power wielded by the Queen of Wands, enabling her to understand the inner workings of nature beyond the material realm. Nature is not a force to be taken lightly. One must approach it with dignity and respect, humility and grace. The Queen of Wands is adept at this, since she is a country woman at heart. The Queen embodies protection, strength, stability, and comfort.

Although she has a mild, romantic nature, the Queen is at times given to theatricality. She has an incredibly optimistic outlook on life, trusting that things will always be taken care of and fall into place as nature sees fit. She has no fear, and her gentleness belies a fierce defensiveness where her friends and loved ones are concerned.

The Queen of Wands is a maternal figure, protecting those she cares about. She sometimes tends to over-manage the lives of those in her sphere of influence but it is only out of love and a feeling of what would be best for them. She can, however, quickly take charge of any situation, and her authoritative stance automatically causes others to fall in line.

Indeed, people look to her for answers and support, since she exudes warmth, wisdom, kindness, and understanding.

The appearance of the Queen of Wands in a reading indicates a person possessing her traits. It implies a connection to the natural and supernatural worlds that will be of great benefit in dealing with others. This card may suggest a need to look on the bright side of life or to take charge of a situation. Matters will easily be resolved if one remains calm and confident.

Reversed Meaning: *Domineering. Vengeful. Self-important. Conniving.*

In a reversed position, the more forceful qualities of the Queen of Wands' personality become degraded. Where the Queen is normally quite authoritative, she becomes dictatorial and exceptionally ambitious. Her romantic nature not only turns to jealously, she is fully capable of plotting and carrying out revenge for any slight. Her natural powers are extremely strong when she is calm. When roused to anger, her wrath knows no bounds. It is not wise to vex the Queen, lest one would like to be hexed.

In this position, the Queen of Wands becomes arrogant, feeling herself to be above others. Rivalry will keep her at odds with others and she is not above malicious behavior to assure that she gets her way.

KING OF WANDS

King of Wands

118

Meaning: *Authoritative. Kind. Generous. Honest. Intelligent.*

The King of Wands is a kind, gentle, nature-loving man. He is handsome and romantic, proud of those in his care. He is an excellent father who dotes on his children and encourages them to be the best they can be. This is a man who leads by example and retains his position of authority through the love and admiration of his subjects.

The King of Wands is an intelligent, well-educated man, capable of making informed decisions although he has a tendency to be a bit hasty. When this card is drawn, the querent needs to make an effort not to rush things even if they sound logical. Hidden facts may surface which could drastically alter what might otherwise be a perfectly sound judgment.

The King of Wands is a good advisor who not only listens well, but who offers sage counsel. Since he is always on the lookout for innovative projects and ideas, he can easily steer someone in the right direction, perhaps opening up exciting new paths for that individual in the process.

When speaking, the intelligence and blatant honesty possessed by the King may cause him to appear blunt and rather outspoken, but this assertiveness is simply him stating his unabashed views. He is used to being in charge of his environs so he does not hesitate to act in a lordly manner. The King of Wands is, in fact, very noble and regal in his bearing anyway, so it is perfectly within his character to take charge of not only a situation, but his surroundings as well.

The appearance of the King of Wands in a reading indicates a person possessing his traits. It may signify that it is time to take control of a situation. Encouragement should be given to subordinates.

Reversed Meaning: *Bossy. Strict. Arrogant. Relinquishment of control.*

The King of Wands in a reversed position may indicate an arrogant and dictatorial personality. His need to have ego and vanity continually fed by others may cause tension that could result in quarrels. The reversed King of Wands is more interested in himself than others and may indicate either the absence of a father or the lack of a father-figure in one's life.

Because of the honesty present in the King's character, this reversal may signify that someone is forthright enough to admit his limitations, stepping down from a task or position that he does not feel qualified to handle. If pride takes over and one is not wise enough to relinquish control, it may result in foolish mistakes and decisions which could easily have been avoided.

 *Cups*

ACE OF CUPS

Ace of Cups

Meaning: *Spiritual and emotional benefits. Happiness. Good news.*

The Ace of Cups is represented by a pure white lotus blossom, symbol of spiritual sacredness. This card signifies new beginnings of a spiritual or emotional nature. Now is the time to relax in the love and comfort of those who understand and support you.

The Ace of Cups may indicate the meeting of new friends, or perhaps a special get-together for old ones. In this case, "the cup is full," and abundance pours from it. Basic necessities are easily taken care of and even more gifts appear seemingly out of nowhere. The Ace signifies new phases of development and a high energy level which make anything possible.

Since the Cups represent emotional and spiritual issues, the Ace may denote a new avenue in one's belief system that could aid in spiritual development. New friends may introduce you to things you had never previously considered and you may experience feelings and thoughts you never knew existed within yourself.

Expect good tidings and happiness every time you turn around! The Universe is giving you precious gifts now. Share them with others as freely as they have been given to you.

Reversed Meaning: *Selfishness. Unappreciative behavior. Unhappiness.*

The Ace of Cups in a reversed position shows an unwillingness to accept the profusion of gifts that have come so readily. This reluctance to be happy and thankful for one's blessings is purely in the mind. There is no reason to be ungrateful for the many outpourings of kindness and generosity being presented.

Selfish, jealous behavior may be preventing the enjoyment of what one has. Material and spiritual gifts mean nothing if they cannot be accepted in the spirit in which they are given. There may be a need to reevaluate one's expectations of self as well as others so that friendship, love, and kindness can be appreciated for what they are.

TWO OF CUPS

Meaning: *Love. Romance. Harmony. Balanced personalities.*

This card was actually inspired by a dream I had in which I was the Queen of the Pirates. I was happily enjoying my command until the crew unceremoniously dumped me overboard. At first I thought they were joking until I saw the ship moving further and further away. My indignation quickly turned to fear as I realized that there was no land in sight and I could not continue to tread water forever.

I was rescued by a merman, who took me to his underwater home. It was love at first sight and there was almost no hesitation on my part when he offered to make me a mermaid. I knew life would be different but I would be able to share it with the one that felt "right." And of course, we lived happily ever after.

I believe it is totally unnecessary to change for a person, especially to remain in his or her good graces. None of us need be something we are not simply in order to impress others. Love should never be founded on what each person is willing to change but rather, what each person is willing to share.

The symbolism of my dream, in reality, points to my consistently choosing the wrong men – the pirates – and mistakenly believing they would behave as I wished. It was only when I was saved by someone totally different yet who I could tell truly loved me, that I was able to be content in love. The merman brought out a calmness in me that I had not previously felt, and I was able to be the person I really was with him, as opposed to the blustering, swaggering pirate queen I was pretending to be before.

The Two of Cups is a card of friendship, romance, and love. It indicates harmonious relationships and well-balanced personalities. It signifies the productive blending of ideas between two partners, business or otherwise. On another level, it may indicate that the querent has found a balance of male and female energies within self, contributing to a contentment and self-acceptance never before realized.

Reversed Meaning: *Misunderstanding. Loss of balance. Love turned bad.*

The Two of Cups in a reversed position suggests that there has been a loss of balance in a relationship, and the individuals involved may be at cross purposes. Since this is such a positive card, the problem might simply be that perceptions are slightly amiss, causing partners to be at odds when it is really unnecessary.

THREE OF CUPS ═══

3 Cups

Meaning: *Friendship. Merriment. Good Fortune. Happy conclusion.*

Three water nymphs joyously gather together to celebrate their friendship. The shell, which represents spiritual gifts and talents, is used to toast their camaraderie and the many things they have in common. More often than not, we are drawn to those who share our interests. Such friendships tend to have an enduring quality as they give a solid footing to the relationship that may not be present with mere acquaintances. This mutual sharing of ideas and information allows for sustained connections with those we call our dearest friends.

Another special aspect of genuine friendship is having a shoulder on which to cry. A best friend understands you better than anyone and will be there to listen and offer advice when you need it most. A true friend is someone you can just sit with quietly, as bonds tend to run so deeply that words are not always necessary.

The Three of Cups signifies friendships and all the joy that accompanies them. It may be indicative of an upcoming social gathering, with all its merriment and revelry. The Three of Cups reminds us to be grateful for all the wonderful friends and blessings we have. The appearance of this card in a reading heralds good fortune. Rejoice in your friendships and know that all good things are available to you now.

Reversed Meaning: *Overindulgence. Gossip. Good things turn unpleasant.*

A reversal of the Three of Cups indicates overindulgence. In a social situation, this could point to the misuse of drugs and alcohol. While enjoyment of life is a delightful thing, one must be careful not to take it to extremes. When individuals get together in groups, they are more prone to do things outside the realm of their normal behavior. Reckless antics could result in harm to others as well as themselves. The Three of Cups in a reversed position warns us to curb unrestrained behavior with friends before a good situation turns bad.

This card may also mean that someone is taking advantage of a friendship. True friends do not manipulate others to serve their own purposes. Gossip is a by-product of the ill treatment of friends that can easily result in the loss of a person normally considered very dear to one's heart.

FOUR OF CUPS

4 Cups

Meaning: *Discontent. Boredom. Spiritual sorrow. Daydreams.*

A lone mermaid rests on a sandbar, taking in the glittering lights of the town that dots the banks of the shore. The treasures lying around her remain virtually unnoticed as she gazes with intrigue at the world so close and yet so far from her own. Is it really so wonderful? A church rises prominently before her. It is obviously a special place for the humans that inhabit the area. What does it all mean? Is it better than her own world?

As humans, it is in our nature to feel that the grass is always greener on the other side of the fence. We have a tendency to perceive different things as special, simply because we do not fully understand them. By the same token, we are often frightened of the things we do not understand.

The mermaid appears to be discontent with the life into which she was born. She wonders if the human world has more to offer, never realizing that humans may feel the same way about the gloriously beautiful world she inhabits.

The Four of Cups is a card of daydreaming – imagining better situations or lifestyles than what we are currently experiencing and wanting more than what we already have or need. This frustration may be caused by anything from a desire for material wealth to a spiritual yearning that has not been satisfied. While there is nothing wrong with daydreams, the discontent that gives rise to them is something that we need to face and conquer.

Reversed Meaning: *Restlessness. Novelty. New opportunities. Possible new relationships.*

A reversal of the Four of Cups encourages us to make productive use of our restless nature by acting on our desires and seeking to learn more about the things that fascinate us. One must remain aware that the novelty of a new experience may quickly wear off, since the grass is *not* always greener on the other side.

Actually *doing* something, or trying something new, is better than always wondering "what if." Things that seemed very tempting and wonderful from afar may prove to be quite a turnoff once they are more fully understood. Yet you lose nothing by *trying* and you will be exposed to new people and ideas that will add to your life experiences. You may even find that your new passion is just what you have been waiting for your entire life!

FIVE OF CUPS

5 Cups

Meaning: *Sorrow. Lament. Sacrifice. Deceit. Disillusionment.*

According to legend, an undine was a female water sprite who could acquire a soul by marrying a human being. If, however, her lover proved unfaithful, the undine had to return to the sea. Many tales have been written about a specific water sprite named Undine, whose lover betrayed her, only to die himself with one last kiss from the water sprite.

This card depicts Undine as she emerges from a waterfall into the exotic realm of human beings. At this point, she expresses all the delight and wonderment of a child upon encountering new realms. Everything to her is enchanting and exciting. She has left behind her previous life, yearning for something more, yet it will only be a matter of time before our world disillusions her as well.

The Five of Cups expresses a sorrow with the way things are without true hope that they will get much better. Joy is fleeting, and disappointment will soon reign once again. All of the things one has strived for could disappear in an instant of deceit and one's sacrifices will all be for naught.

Reversed Meaning: *Hope regained. Relationships with friends and family.*

In a reversed position, the Five of Cups offers a more hopeful outlook. Even if things are not what one expected, a way is found to deal productively with them. Friends and family may help in this endeavor, as they were there all along, whether this was realized or not. Even when we try to distance ourselves from our former existence, it remains with us, providing the background necessary to sustain, and if necessary, reclaim us. We were born into our environs for a reason. It is the past that makes us who we are, the future which makes us what we wish to be.

SIX OF CUPS

6 Cups

Meaning: *New surroundings. Memories. Nostalgia. Discontent.*

A fairy stands before a fountain in her watery domain. Jars from the human world are positioned at her feet, waiting to be filled with the waters of her existence. Perhaps the water fairy has a desire to meld her world with that of humans in order to share her wisdom and experience stimulating new events, or maybe she feels pushed into uniting her kingdom with the ever-encroaching world of humans. Whatever the case, she has a look of consternation on her face, as if she is somewhat unsure about her situation.

The Six of Cups is a card of nostalgia, fond remembrances of the past. As such, it may indicate a discontent with one's present situation. When we are unhappy where we are, it is comforting to think of better days from times gone by. Memories remain with us always, but we must take care not to live in the past.

This card suggests that it is time to move on and try new things. One might consider relocating to a new area or job for a change of scenery. Or, on a lighter note, maybe this would be a good time to redecorate one's living space. Sometimes even the simplest changes can make a world of difference.

Reversed Meaning: *Outworn friendships. Using past experience for future growth.*

A reversal of the Six of Cups suggests that one needs to focus on the future, as the past has outlived its usefulness. We need not disregard our past experiences but sometimes, as our way of living becomes outmoded, we need a change. Even the friendships we carry for so long can outlive their potential. Perhaps an assessment of current circumstances is necessary in order to enlighten one as to the continued significance of existing relationships.

Use the knowledge gained from the past in order to pave the way for the future. We all have unique histories that not only make us who we are but who we wish to be.

SEVEN OF CUPS

7 Cups

Meaning: *Illusion. Fantasy. Self-indulgence in dreams. Hazy thinking.*

Three sirens attempt to lure a passing ship onto the rocks. Sailors long away at sea were easy prey for the deceptive appearance of these dangerous water spirits. It was not uncommon for sailors to jump overboard in hopes of the sensual pleasures they believed awaited them in the arms of beautiful mermaids and sprites. Sometimes, entire ships were dashed upon rocky crags, enticed by the haunting, melodic siren songs.

The Seven of Cups warns of illusory dreams and the danger of giving in to a world of fantasy. Everyone daydreams, but letting such thoughts rule one's waking life and influence one's actions is a dangerous undertaking. While the world of dreams is necessary to the well-being of our minds, letting them cloud one's thinking can be disastrous.

The appearance of this card may indicate self-indulgence in flights of fancy or even decadence in one's everyday life. Living in a world of fantasy may seem appealing but it causes a break down in communications and how one deals with daily events. When our perceptions are skewed, we have difficulty making clear, rational decisions.

This card represents a tendency to imagine how we want things to be, without making any effort in real life to cause our ideas come to pass. The everyday world may seem mundane, and dreams may allow us a temporary escape from it, but only genuine *action* will allow us to accomplish our goals.

Reversed Meaning: *Logical thinking. Will power. Purpose. Objectives accomplished.*

A reversal of the Seven of Cups emphasizes the need for logical thinking and the use of will-power. When we have a goal in mind and the resolve to achieve it, our power is limitless. Our own determination can see us past any stumbling blocks, and our daydreams can urge us on toward the grandiose designs of our imaginations.

EIGHT OF CUPS

8 Cups

Meaning: *Shyness. Disappointment in love. Rejection of material life.*

A naiad stands seductively in her stream, fingering a Jack-in-the-Pulpit, completely aware of the man gazing ardently at her from the trees. Water Fairies can be notoriously dangerous to human men, and this one is no exception. The man may simply be a weary traveler gone to the river's edge in search of water when he spied the lovely nymph, or perhaps his intentions toward this lone and seemingly unprotected beauty are less than honorable. The fickle and deadly nature of the water nymph expresses itself in her eyes. Is she anxious for a new lover or does she wish to drag another human being into the depths of her watery domain?

The Eight of Cups in a reading indicates a tendency toward shyness and modesty. The querent may be yearning after someone who is unreachable, or perhaps is too timid to make a first move or reciprocate advances. This card in its upright position implies disappointment in love, so no amount of trying may be effective.

The watery nature of this card suggests a tendency to spiritual and emotional thoughts, rather than a desire for material possessions. Perhaps this card indicates a need to become more sensitive to a person's spiritual and emotional requirements, rather than physical ones. It is easy to overlook our ethereal natures in favor of our more tangible selves, but all aspects of our character need to be appreciated for us to truly be content.

Reversed Meaning: *Pleasure seeking. New love interest. Joy. Festivities. Success.*

The Eight of Cups in a reversed position suggests that a new love interest may be imminent. This card indicates a time of happiness and pleasure seeking that will be fulfilled. Now is the time to share your joyfulness with others, so that even more will come back to you. Things that interest you will bring great success.

135

NINE OF CUPS

Meaning: *Success. Physical comfort and health. Wishes come true.*

A mermaid happily cavorts among sea anemones which are symbolic of health, protection, foresight, determination, and expectancy. Sometimes sea anemones were seen as a symbol of death and destruction since they represented the souls of drowned sailors, but that thought seems to be far away from the mind of this blissful sea creature.

This is the wish card. Everything one has hoped for is now ready to come true. Physical well-being and peace of mind have paved the way for success that can only be accomplished when one has nothing to fear. Energy is about to reach its zenith, and now is the time to take advantage of all the world has to offer. Nothing is outside the realm of possibility.

Reversed Meaning: *Overindulgence. Possible ill health. Lack of material goods.*

In its reversed position, the Nine of Cups indicates that one has probably had too much of a good thing. Overindulgence is not the best thing for humans as it tends to make us lazy, sluggish, and sometimes even sick. As such, this card implies possible ill health – returning to normal, less extravagant behavior will make a difference.

Just as the sea anemones at times represent death and destruction, a reversal of the Nine of Cups may indicate a loss of material goods. Because of the spiritual and emotional nature of the suit of Cups, this lack of material possessions may be totally self-instigated. One may have reached a point in life where physical possessions and experiences simply do not matter as much as they once did.

TEN OF CUPS

10 Cups

Meaning: *Ecstasy. Inspiration. Happy home life. Loving friends.*

Asrais ecstatically dance about a waterfall in their nighttime realm. These delicate, translucent fairies (also known as Ashrays) keep to the shadowy depths of the waters throughout the day, as exposure to sunlight will turn them to mere puddles. At night, however, they have the freedom to express their exultation in all that is Nature, flowing as freely through the air as they do in the water.

The Ten of Cups is a card of ecstasy. Unlike the Nine of Cups which refers to individual happiness, the Ten encompasses entire groups – friends, family, co-workers, fellow citizens and countrymen, even mankind as a whole.

This is a time of joy for all to revel in, but one must be aware that just as Asrais quickly disappear in the sunlight, this elation may also be fleeting. Most often, the sheer excitement we experience is in the *anticipation* of something wonderful happening. Of course, we are always thrilled when something we hope for finally comes to pass, but afterwards it sometimes feels as if we have nothing left to look forward to.

Still, one mustn't dwell on the negative aspects. This is a time to share all one's love and exuberance with others.

It could indicate holiday festivities, parties, community gatherings, or just a general moment of much-deserved group happiness.

Reversed Meaning: *Debauchery. Betrayal. Family disputes. Loss of friendship.*

A reversal of the Ten of Cups takes ecstasy to the extreme. It suggests debauchery that could result in a problematic situation. This reflects the mind-set of partygoers who have had too much to drink without thought of the consequences of their actions. It is also the attitude of fans who cannot merely be content that a favored team has won an important game. They end up releasing their pent-up excitement in objectionable behavior that can easily turn into a riot.

The Ten of Cups reversed suggests betrayal and arguments. Disputes with friends and family are likely, and they may even result in the termination of a cherished friendship.

PAGE OF CUPS

Page of Cups

Meaning: *Dreamer. Loyal. Kind. Romantic. Sensitive nature.*

The Page of Cups is quite the dreamer! All kinds of fantasies and imaginings fill his head constantly. His nature is idyllic and romantic and his view of the world tends to revolve around his own expectations of it. Unfortunately, this can be problematic for the Page of Cups, as his highly sensitive nature causes him much distress and embarrassment when things turn out far different from what he envisions them to be.

The Page of Cups has a tendency to idealize situations. This, coupled with his romantic nature, makes him apt to view relationships as much more deep and involved than they really are. The Page of Cups craves love and affection and he is easily hurt when his feelings are not reciprocated.

The Page is a pure delight to have as a friend or acquaintance. He easily becomes the life of any party and truly admires all the attention it brings. The sensitive nature of the Page of Cups, combined with his gentle and kind disposition, make for a highly sympathetic, as well as empathetic, individual. He is someone you can talk to who will understand your feelings quite well.

The Page of Cups is an intelligent, thoughtful person who has much to contribute to society. His loyalty knows no bounds, and he is fearless when it comes to protecting those he cares about. He has a profound love for his friends that will never wane.

The appearance of this card in a reading suggests a person with characteristics of the Page of Cups. It may indicate a need to be more sensitive to the feelings of others or to allow oneself the freedom to dream.

Reversed Meaning: *Weakness. Love of sensual pleasures and attention. Heartache.*

The Page of Cups reversed indicates a weak-willed individual who is easily swayed by attention and flattery. His dreamy nature and idealism make for a rather melodramatic personality. Even his manner of dress and other tastes evince his dramatic flair. The Page of Cups loves sensual pleasures and tries to the best of his abilities to live a life of luxury.

In its reversal, this card may signify great heartache. Even in its upright position, the Page of Cups symbolizes love in its formative stages rather than the deep, abiding love one hopes for. In its reversal, the Page of Cups stands for unrequited love and longing.

PRINCESS OF CUPS

Princess of Cups

Meaning: *Charming. Friendliness. Meetings. Possible journey by water.*

The Princess of Cups is a lovely individual. She is charming, friendly, persuasive, and constantly surrounded by admirers. Because of her natural affability, she makes an excellent salesperson. People instinctively believe and trust her. The Princess gathers and retains friends quite easily. She loves peace and harmony in relationships and she can be depended upon whenever someone needs her.

The Princess of Cups is so attractive that she never lacks for admirers. Since she has so many to choose from, she may decide to play the field before finally settling on someone with whom she wishes to really share her life. The Princess is romantic and outgoing, enjoying all kinds of social activities. While she would never intentionally lead someone on, nevertheless that is bound to happen. Her natural friendliness may often be misread as flirting by those drawn to her charismatic personality.

The Princess of Cups is artistic and takes pleasure in expressing that side of her character. Her clothing, jewelry, and residence all reflect the things she finds most beautiful. One should not be surprised to see her home décor change frequently as the artist in the Princess of Cups is always seeking a creative outlet.

The appearance of this card in a reading may indicate upcoming social events where the innate skills of the Princess of Cups will be of value. A journey by water may be in the offing, although there is the possibility that water may somehow hamper a planned journey.

Reversed Meaning: *Seduction. Sensuality. Deception.*

The Princess of Cups in a reversed position suggests a seductive personality that may be given to deceit in order to accomplish her goals. Lying is indicated, so someone may be withholding pertinent information to intentionally lead others astray.

Another aspect to the reversal of this card is that invitations may be rescinded or not given at all. Someone may simply not be in a mood to celebrate or be around a lot of people at this time.

QUEEN OF CUPS

Queen of Cups

Meaning: *Kind. Shy. Sensitive. Romantic. Self-indulgent.*

The Queen of Cups is a beautiful, gentle creature, given to romantic flights of fancy. She has the soul of an artist with a great love for peace and harmony. The Queen shapes her world to correspond to the way she feels it should be; therefore, much of what she chooses to see is based on illusion. This is not only a way of life for the Queen of Cups; it is also a defense mechanism that protects her from a world that does not measure up to her ideals. Still, it enables the Queen to see the best in everyone, most especially those she considers dear to her heart.

The Queen of Cups prefers to live a life of luxury and foregoes the use of common sense where financial matters are concerned. She is an intelligent person, but one who consciously chooses to live in her own little world, regardless of the fact that troubles may surround her. Her self-indulgent, frivolous personality is a bit at odds with her genuine sensitivity and caring for others.

Like the emblematic seashell of water she holds, the Queen of Cups has many spiritual gifts and talents to share with others. She is an empathetic and sympathetic person who would take the weight of the world on her shoulders, if she allowed such negative influences into her life. She is basically a dreamer who prefers to make the world as beautiful and gentle as she is, and her inherent graceful nature flows freely out to everyone she meets.

The appearance of this card in a reading indicates someone with personality traits of the Queen of Cups. A kind and gentle nature allows one to see the best in others yet keeps one rather introverted. This card suggests a slightly frivolous nature, albeit a very caring one.

Reversed Meaning: *Unreliable. Insecure. Codependent. Seductive.*

Reversed, the Queen of Cups shows a less generous side to her nature. She becomes far more self-centered and less interested in the welfare and feelings of others. This behavior may stem from insecurities she feels about herself, which cause her to act in a codependent manner. At this point she may feel the need to have a protector, although, in reality, she is the one who bears the strength of the relationship.

In a reversed position, this card indicates that the Queen is not above using seduction to lure others to do her bidding. Because she cares primarily about her own pleasure, the Queen will willingly, if unintentionally, sacrifice others just to get what she wants.

Although the Queen of Cups is normally a very caring friend, she may not be reliable, depending upon her mood. She may start out with the best of intentions, but even a slight emotional shift can upend her world and cause her to suddenly change her mind without the slightest concern for others.

KING OF CUPS

King of Cups

Meaning: *Kind. Thoughtful. Helpful. Calm and powerful leader.*

Triton, ruler of the sea, holds forth a blue goblet that cannot help but overflow with the emotional and spiritual waters of his domain. Like all mermen, Triton is a wise and gifted teacher. Legendary sea beings such as Triton and Poseidon have reputations as great scientists and mathematicians. Unlike many land and sky deities, the sea gods happily share their vast wealth of knowledge with human beings for whom they feel a deep attachment and respect.

The King of Cups represents an excellent leader – calm, rational, and sensitive to his subjects. He would make an excellent clergyman, doctor, scientist, artist or teacher, as he feels that his knowledge and abilities are meant to be shared with others both for their own benefit and to make them better human beings.

The King of Cups is a deep man – he has thoughts, talents, and abilities that often remain hidden simply because as a leader, he must exert a certain amount of authority. Exposing his more creative and thoughtful side could hinder his ability to retain control in a society that does not prize those qualities above the dominance of leadership. Still, the King is a fatherly figure and a great nurturer. Anyone who knows him realizes how much he is to be admired.

The appearance of the King of Cups in a reading indicates a kind, thoughtful, and powerful personality. It may signify the need to apply one's intellectual and artistic gifts for the betterment of society.

Reversed Meaning: *Violent. Cunning. Powerful. Duplicitous behavior.*

The goldfish swimming around Triton represent spiritually confining beliefs or conditions, and as such, they reveal the more negative side of the King of Cups. Because of his sheer intelligence, the King can be exceedingly cunning and crafty, twisting words and situations to suit his own purposes.

The reversal of this card suggests that the King of Cups may be underhanded and double-dealing in his affairs. Because of the enormous power and influence he wields, this can be very detrimental to the faith and trust others put in him. The King of Cups is not a figure one should rile as his violence is unbounded when his anger is roused.

 *Rings*

ACE OF RINGS

Ace of Rings

Meaning: *Beginnings of prosperity. Business venture. Onset of good fortune.*

The Ace of Rings depicts a fairy relaxing on a ring of violets which are the occult symbol of Twilight. Twilight is that magical time when the world of Faery traverses our third-dimensional realm, bringing with it the endless possibilities of time and space. Because fairies are not confined to matter as humans are, they have more control over their own existences and sometimes those of others.

The violet also is a symbol of humility and simplicity, which are two character traits highly prized by the denizens of Faery. Fairies typically favor individuals who are hard-working, humble, and down-to-earth. The Ace of Rings embodies the gifts and happiness fairies take pleasure in showering on people they deem worthy.

Rings represent the Tarot suit more commonly referred to as Coins or Pentacles; therefore, the suit of Rings represents financial matters, as well as issues of general health and happiness. The Ace of Rings in a reading indicates that a time of good fortune and prosperity is on its way. This is a time for new beginnings in business ventures, when one's hard work begins to pay off. It may also indicate an inheritance or other financial windfall.

The Fairy Ring is a blessed place where inhabitants of Faery gather to celebrate life. The Ace of Rings symbolizes the beginning of all good things, and the sheer delight and energy that accompany new activities.

Reversed Meaning: *Greed. Materialism. Fool's gold.*

A reversal of the Ace of Rings cannot really mitigate the inherent happiness and good fortune of this card, although its fundamental nature could be taken to extremes. This may be seen as an overabundance of wealth causing one to become greedy and materialistic. As far as health concerns go, excellent physical condition may cause one to become lax in his habits – perhaps overeating or taking unnecessary risks, simply out of the belief that nothing adverse could possibly happen.

Another aspect of this card may be the desire to hold back when there is no need. Fear of losing whatever one has may prompt the urge to hoard items, even though there is no reason for such behavior. One may feel that the gifts he has received are too good to be true – like fool's gold – and that they cannot be utilized, lest they fade away like fairy money turning back into leaves.

TWO OF RINGS

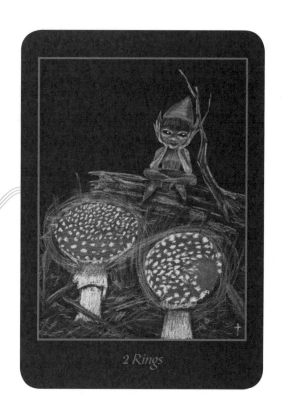

2 Rings

Meaning: *Juggling two things at once. Harmony. Confusion.*

The Two of Rings is represented by one of the *Buachaileen*, or "herding boys," mischievous fairies who wear pointed red caps and like to play pranks on animals and shepherds just for fun. Here, one happily sits atop a twig fallen from a tree, while the sign for eternity envelops the two mushrooms before him.

The Two of Rings signifies the ability to juggle two things at once, although the duality symbolized in this card indicates that these things may be at odds with one another. Still, in its upright position, this card suggests that the querent should easily be able to maintain control of the situation. The mushrooms pictured here symbolize the benefit that results from a seemingly negative factor, and the infinity sign surrounding them indicates that this is a perpetual issue we all have to deal with. It is up to each individual whether to allow simultaneous experiences to cause confusion and conflict or whether to work in concert with the situation, thereby producing harmony.

Reversed Meaning: *Difficulty handling too many things at once. Discouraging message.*

The Two of Rings reversed suggests difficulty in dealing with too many things at once. Because of the physical nature of the suit of Rings, this indicates problems with work, finances, and possibly even health. The querent may be overwhelmed with responsibility both at home and work. There may be difficulty in paying bills or making ends meet, and the ensuing stress may cause health problems. One may receive a discouraging message.

THREE OF RINGS

3 Rings

Meaning: *Material gain through hard work. Skill rewarded. Working with others.*

The Three of Rings portrays a dwarf successfully working at his job, mining for precious gems. This card in its upright position indicates material gain through hard work, particularly work done in concert with others.

Dwarves are known for their skill in many areas, most especially as miners and metallurgists, and they tend to work quite well together. The Three of Rings suggests that work is accomplished more easily and to a greater degree when done with the assistance of others.

In South Central Europe, Dwarf fairies known as *Knockers* labor in mines and caves. They enjoy playing games, but they also care for respectful miners by knocking – either to point out a rich vein, or to warn miners of impending danger. This shows a penchant for helping not only close friends and associates but even those one does not especially know. The finest things mankind accomplishes are not for selfish reasons, but for the greater good.

The Three of Rings in a reading indicates success achieved through hard work. It implies skills rewarded owing to the collective efforts of everyone involved in a project.

Reversed Meaning: *Mediocre workmanship. Lack of ambition. Fixation or anxiety about money.*

A reversal of the Three of Rings indicates a lack of ambition which may reveal itself through mediocre workmanship. When one cares nothing for what he is doing, he rarely takes the time to see that it is done to the best of his ability. This lack of interest benefits no one. If a person has no concern for what he is doing, then it is time to find something he feels more passionate about.

The Three of Rings in a reversed position may also suggest either a fixation on money or anxiety about it. Taking a job for the money it provides is not as fulfilling as having a job one enjoys, even if the pay is less. We all have concerns over our financial situations but money cannot fix everything in our lives. While comfort is important, so is happiness. When we are unhappy, both our health and our mental outlook are adversely affected, and then we in turn begin to adversely affect those closest to us. It is time to consider what one deems most important – money or contentment.

FOUR OF RINGS

Meaning: *Kindness. Generosity. Protection. Miserliness. Fear of loss.*

The Four of Rings depicts a fairy guarding blossoms on her redbud tree. Like all of nature, the redbud will go through various stages of seasonal growth and decay. No matter how much the little fairy looks after her beloved blossoms, they will still go through their natural process and fall from the tree.

The Four of Rings suggests the kindness and generosity of spirit to care deeply for something and yet share it with others. Still, this card implies overprotection of one's wealth or material goods that amounts to miserliness. The fear of losing what one holds dear encourages the need to hoard possessions even though nothing in the material world is ours to keep forever.

This card is a reminder to freely share the gifts one has, rather than keeping them to oneself. All of nature is cyclical, and that includes every material object on this planet. Nothing in the physical is permanent. The more we give of a material nature, the more we get back of a spiritual nature.

Reversed Meaning: *Obstacles. Opposition. Possible loss of earthly possessions.*

The Four of Rings in a reversed position indicates constraints that keep one from attaining his goal. These obstacles are probably not on behalf of the querent. Rather, opposition comes from an outside source that refuses to let go of something, be it money, time, or self. Until someone is ready to give a little, nothing is likely to change.

A reversal of the Four of Rings also suggests the possible loss of earthly belongings. When we hold on to things too tightly, they have a tendency to slip through our fingers. A certain level of detachment from material possessions is necessary in order to achieve a balance between one's physical and spiritual natures.

FIVE OF RINGS

Meaning: *Anxiety. Loneliness. Desolation. Despair. Possible illness.*

Traditionally, Samhain is a time when the gates of Faery open wide, allowing that world to easily cross into ours, and vice-versa. Shortly after Samhain, however, the doors to the Faery realm swing shut to block off the impending winter, limiting fairy activities in our world until the approach of warmer weather.

The Five of Rings depicts a fairy who reveled a bit too long in the world of mortals, locked out of her precious home. The fairy appears to be quite frightened, unsure of what will become of her if she is not allowed entry back into the land she loves so dearly. Snowflakes fall down on her, heralding the approach of winter. She knows the longer it takes to reenter the gates of Faery, the more likely she will have to spend the harsh season in a world to which she is not accustomed.

The Five of Rings represents anxiety. One's worst fears may come true. This card indicates hard times, loneliness, depression, suffering, and the general grief and despair that accompany such difficulties. Illness is possible, perhaps even brought on by continual worry. Bear in mind that when one has reached rock-bottom, the only direction to go is up.

Reversed Meaning: *Stability may not last. New interest in spirituality. Lesson in charity.*

A reversal of the Five of Rings suggests that even while circumstances appear to be improving, things are still on shaky ground. New employment may not last. A problematic relationship that one thought was mended may still fall apart. Remission from an illness may be fleeting. While all of these situations seem untenable, one must not give up hope or the ability to move on. Everything we experience in life contributes to our development as individuals.

The Five of Rings reversed may also signify a new or renewed interest in spirituality. When the physical world gets to be too much to handle, human beings often reflect upon their more spiritual nature, which is a good thing. This focus on our souls, rather than our bodies, enables us to become more understanding and accepting of others. Consequently, one may see the joy and satisfaction to be found in charitable acts toward others.

SIX OF RINGS

o Rings

Meaning: *Kindness. Generosity. Gifts given are received back in greater amounts.*

While meditating one day, I was surprised by the sudden appearance of this gnome and his comfortable dwelling. Just as in the picture, the gnome was graciously offering me a freshly-made pumpkin pie *that I could smell!* Even though it all happened in a flash, I felt the warmth of his cozy tree-root home – from the dirt floor with straw scattered about to soften it, to the dry, cool wood walls of his abode. I felt totally drawn into his world as a welcome guest.

Gnomes are typically countryside or woodland dwellers who make their homes among the root systems of trees. They are considered a major earth elemental because of their love of nature and their desire to remain at peace and protect all of the earth's creatures. They have only a few natural enemies – owls and cats, primarily – but generally care for all forest creatures, especially the wounded and dying.

Gnomes are kind and gentle, with a jovial and loving nature. Although they are of Faery, some humans have had the good fortune to actually behold or receive gifts from them. They are not above putting a person in his place, but for the most part they simply try to aid the world in attaining the peace they know is possible.

The Six of Rings signifies kindness and a generosity of spirit. The ability to give selflessly and make others happy is a gift beyond measure. Whatever we give out of love and selflessness returns to us in even greater amounts. It behooves us humans to try to act more like the gentle, happy, and loving gnomes. If we did, our world would become a much better place to live.

Reversed Meaning: *Bribery. Unfair dealings. Injustice. Miserliness. Threatened prosperity.*

A reversal of the Six of Rings also suggests the giving of gifts, but in the form of bribery rather than true generosity. Others act as friends, simply to get something they want. One's prosperity is threatened by the selfish desires of others. This may even relate to a divorce case or problems with the settlement of an estate.

The Six of Rings reversed implies injustice done to others in the name of greed. It also indicates a miserly nature that is not willing to share with others.

SEVEN OF RINGS

7 Rings

Meaning: *Gain or reward through hard work. Money. Waiting patiently.*

Leprechauns are tricksters that delight in playing pranks on humans. However, mischievous as they are, if approached with respect, they can actually be quite helpful. Leprechauns are basically solitary creatures, known for guarding pots of gold. Lore has it that if one can catch a Leprechaun, he will be given the crock of gold and three wishes. Leprechauns are not easy to catch, as they are prone to fading completely from one's grasp. Even if one does manage to capture a Leprechaun, he still has his work cut out for him. Leprechauns will seek to win back their gold through riddles and word games, and they can easily prevail over humans who then lose the both the crock of gold and the three wishes.

The Seven of Rings depicts a rather sinister-looking Leprechaun guarding his pot of gold. One must wonder if the Leprechaun is planning a trick. Perhaps he is willing to let go of his pot of gold, only to laugh at his clever joke later when the gold coins all turn to leaves like the ones scattered beside his cauldron.

The Seven of Rings suggests that if one is patient and tends well to his projects, they will bear fruit. There is an element of uncertainty associated with the upright position of this card that is much worse in its reversal. Still, hard work will be rewarded, not only with money but with a great sense of satisfaction over a job well done.

Reversed Meaning: *Impatience. Anxiety. Setbacks. Loss or small gain after great effort.*

In its reversed position, the Seven of Rings indicates impatience and anxiety over a project or other matter. When we take too little time to nurture things properly, they seldom reach a healthy level of maturity. Setbacks may prevent things from running as smoothly as one might hope. Worrying over matters does not help, either. It only serves to create negative energy that will benefit nothing.

Another aspect of the reversal is that even enormous amounts of hard work come to naught. Like chasing a Leprechaun and having him slip through one's fingers, whatever one has cultivated long and hard fades away. Even if some gain is made in a project, one will still be left wondering if it was all worth the effort.

EIGHT OF RINGS

8 Rings

Meaning: *Skill. Hard work. Apprenticeship. Learning. Attaining a goal.*

Elves are Faery Folk who are normally kind and helpful to humans, especially those in need. The tale of the Elves and the Shoemaker aptly portrays the benevolent nature of elves, as they willingly give their assistance to an unwitting shoemaker who was too poor to afford to do much with the small amount of leather in his possession. For quite some time, the elves entered the shoemaker's shop at night, making shoes from the leather he cut during the day. Finally, after becoming rather wealthy from the sale of the shoes they found sitting out each morning, the shoemaker and his wife determined to discover how shoes were being made as they slept. One night they stayed awake and spied on the shop, only to behold two naked elves, happily engaged in their work. Feeling grateful, yet sorry for the unclothed state of the elves, the shoemaker and his wife made tiny outfits for them to wear. The next night, when the elves spotted the clothing, they quickly donned it and cheerfully cavorted about the room. After that, the shoemaker and his wife never saw the elves again, but their good fortune continued.

The Eight of Rings refers to skill in one's work, but primarily at an apprenticeship stage. There is still much to learn, even though one's talent is obvious. Hard work and patience will ultimately allow one to achieve his goals.

Reversed Meaning: *Laziness. Lack of ambition. Unreliability. Improper use of skills.*

A reversal of the Eight of Rings indicates laziness and a lack of ambition. When one does not enjoy his work, his lack of interest often shows itself through unreliable behavior such as coming to work late, doing a poor job, pushing things off on others, etc.

The Eight of Rings reversed also suggests the improper use of one's skills. Greed may be a primary factor for using one's abilities for the wrong reasons. In some versions of the above tale, the shoemaker becomes greedy and happily allows the elves to continue doing his work, while he takes off to enjoy himself only to be punished by the elves, who refuse to assist him any further. One needs to be grateful for the assistance offered him, and learn from what others have to teach.

NINE OF RINGS

Meaning: *Contentment. Security. Enjoyment of life. Possible inheritance.*

Wilde Frauen, or "Wild Women," are diminutive female forest spirits who represent all ages of women, from childhood through old age. They live among the tree roots deep in forests and dress in foliage of the current season. Due to its close association with nature, the Nine of Rings indicates a "green thumb," as well as a general love of the natural world.

Here, a young Wilde Frauen plays merrily with bubbles. Although bubbles symbolically tend to represent the negative aspects of one's existence, life is what one makes of it. This fairy shows that even the worst situations in life cannot take away from our happiness. If bubbles are troubles, she laughs at them, seeing them as small playthings that she can easily burst if she so chooses.

The Nine of Rings signifies contentment and the happiness that it brings. Hard work and perseverance have paid off and it is time to relax and enjoy the beautiful things life has to offer.

This card represents security and the ability to rest at ease with one's financial situation. An inheritance is possible, although it is not necessary to afford the monetary stability that is already inherent in this card – it would simply be icing on the cake. Take pleasure in the peace, happiness, and well being the Nine of Rings offers. You have earned it.

Reversed Meaning: *Possible loss or theft. Deceit. Threat to safety. Overindulgence.*

In its reversed position, the Nine of Rings suggests that one may lose material comforts. Because of the deceit implied by this reversal, loss may be due to theft of one's property. Be wary of health and safety at this time.

A reversal also indicates that one has grown so accustomed to the good things in life that overindulgence in them has become the norm. By the same token, one may not appreciate all the benefits he has earned or else fears to take advantage of a much-deserved rest after a great deal of hard work.

TEN OF RINGS

Meaning: *Home. Family. Stability. Legacy. Financial prosperity.*

The Ten of Rings depicts two fairies resting comfortably together, hand-in-hand on a plant in their abode. Life is good because they have their home and their health. Life is complete because they have each other.

The Ten of Rings represents the love of home and family. Security and stability accompany this card, especially in regard to strong relationships and a good family name. The familial aspect of this card may express itself through an interest in one's lineage and trying to research family history. There may be an inheritance or work to be done regarding a will.

This card is more than the culmination of prosperity suggested by the suit of Rings. It concerns those we have around us, who love us and will always be there for us. They share in our wealth of happiness. Health and success remain with us as long as we are content and share our joy with those we love.

Reversed Meaning: *Family problems. Indolence. Insecurity. Loss of fortune.*

A reversal of the Ten of Rings suggests that there may be family problems or misfortune. Quarrels may ensue from issues of inheritance or family relationships. Most problems arise due to a feeling of insecurity – either financial or emotional.

Because the Ten of Rings follows the good fortune and well-deserved rest of the Nine of Rings, its reversal heralds a downhill slide in fortunes. One may have become lazy and unwilling to work in order to preserve the family fortune or health may suffer because of family arguments.

PAGE OF RINGS

Page of Rings

Meaning: *Scholarly. Inquisitive. Serious. Open to new ideas.*

The Page of Rings is a quiet, studious type of person, highly inquisitive and attentive to her surroundings. Because the Suit of Rings represents the more material aspects of life, the Page is apt to investigate the world through its relation to nature, understanding and accepting only the more tangible characteristics of existence.

The Page of Rings has a rather serious nature, observing everything. In this card, the Page is seen pondering dewdrops on a spider web, symbolic of the spiritual touch woven through all the complexities of life. For all her earnestness, the Page has a very open mind and is willing to listen to any line of reasoning another has to offer, knowing that she may learn something in the process.

The Page of Rings in a reading indicates a kind, generous, and vigilant person with a close affinity to nature and a willingness to learn from it. Scholarly pursuits are probable, as a search for knowledge of the physical world is of the utmost import to the Page.

This card in a reading may also suggest the need to be more observant, perhaps taking fresh notice of the environment and trying to learn more about it. Keep an open mind and react to situations in a way that will benefit the earth and all her creatures.

Reversed Meaning: *Lack of focus. Rebelliousness. Attachment to material objects. Wastefulness.*

The Page of Rings reversed indicates a lack of focus. This could take the form of doing poorly at school or work or foregoing such obligations altogether. Because of this attitude, the Page would most likely be considered a rebel, flouting authority. In reality, however, the Page just needs to be exposed to something in a way that will hold her interest and provide the motivation to continue learning.

A reversal of this card may suggest an attachment to material objects and a love of luxury with no real thought for the environment. Because of this, a general wastefulness may ensue, compounding the problems our Mother Earth endures daily.

PRINCESS OF RINGS

Princess of Rings

Meaning: *Trustworthy. Patient. Skillful. Love of nature.*

The Princess of Rings is a calm, down-to-earth person that can be relied on at any time. She is trustworthy and patient with a deep and abiding love for nature. Here, the Princess is seen admiring a circlet of roses. She has an innate appreciation for all the treasures the world has to offer, from the most magnificent to the most mundane. What others find boring or ugly intrigues the Princess as much as things that most people consider to be truly beautiful.

The Princess of Rings is a highly skillful and inventive person. Her attention to the details and workings of nature add to her knowledge of design, so she is able to create objects that are quite useful as well as attractive. She is an active personality and has a need to create constantly. She puts her abilities to good use and is a real asset to anyone who needs her help.

The Princess is very methodical and dependable. Because of this, she makes an excellent partner for those who wish to feel secure. Some people may find her character traits ordinary and unexciting but one would be hard-pressed to find a more faithful and loving companion.

The appearance of the Princess in a reading suggests a person with her character traits. This card may indicate a need to pay better attention to one's health. It may also signify a journey by land.

Reversed Meaning: *Irresponsible. Timid. Materialistic. Indolence.*

In its reversal, the Princess of Rings suggests a person so caught up in the physical world that emotional and spiritual issues become neglected. This focus on the material world may be caused either by a desire to accomplish and gain more in the physical or by overindulgence in the gifts the material world has to offer. Either way, this obsession with the material world may take its toll by causing ill health and a feeling of discontent.

The Princess of Rings reversed may indicate a person with a timid nature who is more comfortable around animals and nature than people. She may be given to indolence, without a care for the needs of anyone else. Others may see her as irresponsible and as unpleasant company.

QUEEN OF RINGS

Queen of Rings

Meaning: *Intelligence. Generosity. Hospitality. Stability.*

The Queen of Rings is a generous, loving soul. She is highly intelligent and creative, and more than willing to share her knowledge and skills. She sets an excellent example for others, who admire everything about her.

The Queen of Rings loves company and delights in indulging her guests any way that she can. Her home is immaculate, yet comfortable. She derives great joy from having people visit, and every meal she prepares is a veritable feast. The Queen has never met a stranger and everyone is welcome in her presence.

The Queen of Rings loves nature, and takes special pleasure in its simplest aspects. The wildflowers she sees and talks to while out walking will more than likely end up displayed on her kitchen table where everyone else can see and enjoy them as much as she does. The Queen is likely to have many indoor plants as well as a garden she tends to carefully and lovingly.

The Queen of Rings is pictured with her hawk familiar. Hawks are known for their acute perception and the ability for quick discernment. Like the hawk, the Queen can easily make out what is going on all around her and she uses this ability when dealing with others. She is well aware what those around her are thinking and feeling and she does her best to accommodate them.

The Queen of Rings is a stable personality, with a great deal of common sense and good-natured humor. She is a very charitable person, always giving of herself, not only monetarily but physically and spiritually as well. The Queen realizes how blessed she is with prosperity and she does not hesitate to share her abundance of good fortune.

The appearance of this card in a reading suggests someone with character traits like those of the Queen of Rings. It reflects a love of everything in nature, from plants to people, and the desire to provide for their care.

Reversed Meaning: *Neglectful. Dependent. Suspicious. Treacherous.*

A reversal of the Queen of Rings indicates a stubborn and suspicious personality that is wont to cause trouble. Her discontent may stem from a fear of privation or a fear of failure. Because of these fears, she may allow herself to become dependent on others, expecting them to care for her in ways she believes she cannot do herself. The Queen is pictured holding a turtle, symbolic of her fear of facing responsibility or reality.

Although the Queen may turn to others for support, she is unwilling to give any herself and may even go so far as to offend or betray the very people who extend their kindness to her. Because she feels she can rely on others for whatever she needs, the Queen may become neglectful and slovenly, unappreciative of what she has.

KING OF RINGS

King of Rings

Meaning: *Industry. Financial security. Intelligence. Stability. Loyalty.*

The King of Rings is represented here by the Oak King – a being considered more than Fairy, but less than a god. Admired by all denizens of Faery, the Oak King rules during the waxing of the year from Yule-tide to Midsummer, when most fairies prefer to stay within the boundaries of their own realm.

The appearance of the King of Rings in a reading indicates a leader of business and industry. He is someone highly gifted in mathematics and science that can put his knowledge and expertise to exceptional use. The King commands respect and it is freely given by his subordinates since he is fundamentally a very kind, just, and generous person.

The King of Rings has a great fondness for the outdoors and for material pleasures in general. He likes to play as hard as he works, and he enjoys the company of those he loves. The King of Rings represents a married man, most likely with quite a few children. His family adores him, and he provides well for them.

The King of Rings is a steadfast and loyal person, one who can be depended upon for anything from the gravest matters to the most mundane. The King has a big heart and he willingly imparts his advice to those who seek it.

Reversed Meaning: *Materialism. Abuse of power. Disrespect for nature. Vice.*

The King of Rings reversed indicates a powerful individual who over-indulges in materialism. He may be a business leader who takes advantage of the Earth and her natural resources, abusing the land with no regard for those who would benefit from the very resources he seeks to destroy.

A reversal of the King of Rings suggests a proclivity for gluttony, and his health may suffer due to his physical appetites. In this position, the King becomes perverted and subject to all kinds of vice. He may appear slow and stupid, but he is dangerous when roused to anger.

Conclusion

Thank you for taking this journey into the Twilight Realm. Hopefully, it has provided some enlightenment and drawn you closer to the world of Faery. Never forget fairies and other spirits are always close at hand, willing to help if you just acknowledge them and show appreciation for the natural world they tend to so carefully.

The fairies entrusted this Tarot deck to me in the hope of communicating their feelings to others. The best way to give back to them is to love and care for the earth as much as they do, since it is not only our home – it is their home as well. Simply walking around in nature and taking time to stop and smell the roses will get you on your way to communing with the fairies.

Many excellent books exist on the subject of fairy lore, and I highly recommend researching them and expanding your knowledge of these precious beings that influence our lives on a daily basis. As you study them, the fairies will realize your intentions and try to teach you even more on their own. If you have any questions or comments about this Tarot deck, the author may be contacted at www. twilightrealm.us.

About the Author/Artist

Beth Wilder is a tarot enthusiast who has been fortunate to combine her great love of Faery and her passion for drawing for this deck and book set.